GREAT PLANTS
FOR
COOL PLACES

GREAT PLANTS FOR COOL PLACES

John Bracken

Drawings by Carol Carlson

STEIN AND DAY/*Publishers*/**New York**

First published in 1983
Copyright © 1983 by John Bracken
All rights reserved
Designed by Louis A. Ditizio
Printed in the United States of America
STEIN AND DAY/*Publishers*/Scarborough House
Briarcliff Manor, N.Y. 10510

Library of Congress Cataloging in Publication Data
Bracken, John, 1927–
    Great plants for cool places.

    Includes index.
    I.   House plants.   I.   Title.
SB419. B69   635.9′65   80-5406
ISBN 0-8128-2721-X
ISBN 0-8128-6064-0 (pbk.)

CONTENTS

Introduction

When it's cold outside it may well be cold inside too for the next several years, what with the high cost of energy. What can you do to have beautiful plants in your house or apartment to warm up the home with cheer? There is an answer: Grow cool plants!—those that thrive in chilly temperatures. And there are hundreds of varieties from many plant groups—Orchids, Bromeliads, Begonias for example—that do just fine at 45° to 50°F. If you can take it, so can they. These plants are no more expensive than temperamental tropicals and some of them are more beautiful.

Not all of our houseplants come from the tropics—indeed, few of them do. Most of our plants are native to the temperate zones where growing-season nighttime temperatures often reach down to 45° or even 40°F. Orchids such as Coelogyne and Odontoglossums grow at 8,000 feet where it can be very cold at night. Many of the lovely South African bulbs such as Agapanthus need coolness to bloom and a host of leafy beauties like it chilly. Your indoor garden can be as pretty as it is in midsummer heat if you know which plants to grow and that's what this book is all about. It will also tell you how to protect plants you already have that need warmth and how to have a fine indoor garden no matter what the season or the price of energy.

Plants do make a difference in a home and with gasoline prices as

high as they are more of us are likely to spend more of our time
there so why not have lovely plants to look at and live with. Here
are over 100 very pretty plants that will provide color and beauty
indoors in the most chilling situations to warm your soul and bring
solace to your quivering heart. And some fine drawings so you will
know what you grow.

John Bracken

GREAT PLANTS
FOR
COOL PLACES

1
Plants From Above and Below

Although it's true that a great many plants are native to tropical countries which have warm and even hot days and nights, many other plants grow in temperate and subtropical zones, where the nighttime growing-season temperature may drop to 40 degrees. For example, ginger and banana plants are strictly tropical and so need heat, but such popular plants as orchids and Dieffenbachias thrive in subtropical areas. And hundreds of plants originate from really cold places; these plants grow in locales where evening temperatures are extremely chilly.

In their exotic native lands—South America, Mexico, Africa, Asia, and elsewhere—plants grow at various altitudes: Some thrive on the low forest floor; others (epiphytic), such as orchids, grow higher up, in trees; and many grow in the mountains, at elevations of two to five thousand feet or more. As the elevation goes up the temperatures come down, and some sorts of plants have managed to adapt to almost every climatic condition. The secret of growing plants indoors is to match a plant to the conditions in your home. With energy so costly this means that in winter your plants will be subject to cooler surroundings than in years past. It is senseless to accommodate your plants at the expense of your pocket—and it isn't necessary.

Even when heating costs were low I always believed that plants should live in the conditions you have to offer them. That means

3

exercising care in plant selection. I rarely have to labor over my plants; they grow well because I simply use a little geography when selecting them.

ℐ ℐ The Lessons of Experience

Several years ago, when I lived in Chicago, I became intrigued with Bromeliads, Begonias, Orchids, and other plants. I believed that the plants needed a rain forest atmosphere and so I tried to simulate these conditions in my apartment. My landlord will attest that the walls peeled, the windows corroded from humidity, and his temper flared. (I, of course, made the necessary repairs.) I was trying to mate plants to my frigid apartment, and that was unwise.

By the time I moved to California I had learned that some plants did need warmth most of the time *but many did not*—it all depended on the plant. I started growing plants that were appropriate to my living conditions. In northern California, nights are cool, usually dropping to 40° or 45°. Indoor temperatures vary from 50° to 65°F (somewhat less now because of high fuel costs). I've found it wise to grow the types of Orchids, Bromeliads, Begonias, and other varieties of plants that like the cool conditions I can offer them. I don't grow heat-loving species like Gesneriads, or gingers —trying to cultivate these plants would mean altering my indoor conditions and raising my fuel bills. Anyway, 75°F day and night is just too hot for me and my family. So my plants live with me; I don't reduce my comfort for them, and I don't ask them to try to compromise for me. All indoor gardeners who want to grow houseplants for fun and pleasure rather than as a chore should do the same.

ℐ ℐ ℐ ℐ

♫ ♫ Plants and Their Selection

Plants come from all over the world, from varying climates, but basically you can break down the temperature categories as the English did decades ago—warm, intermediate, and cool. Warm means 75°-78°F by day; intermediate 65°-75°F; and cool 58°-65°F, with a drop of approximately 10 degrees at night. Most homes these days can be characterized as intermediate or cool, and so the plants you select for home growing should fit these conditions.

It is often safe to disregard any information you received from plant shops and other purveyors recommending that this or that plant needs extreme warmth—few plants do. In fact, heat can kill many orchids. I myself lost several good orchids a few years ago during a ten-day hot spell, with temperatures near the 100s. It is true that in lower temperatures and humidities plants cannot and will not grow as rapidly or lushly as they do outdoors in their native habitats, so do not try to force their growth with excess feeding and watering. Let nature take its course. Yes, less light and warmth means slower growth, but so what? You will still have beautiful plants. Plant cultivation indoors is not a mysterious process; almost anyone can grow Orchids, Bromeliads, Vallotas, Velthemias, as well as other splendid plants. Wise selection and common-sense care will result in a bountiful yield of greenery.

♫ ♫ Cool Plants

Native to the higher elevations, Orchids, Bromeliads, bulbs, and other plants thrive in a cool environment. In fact, with too much heat they seldom survive in the home. These are the plants you should grow in energy-saving rooms where you've reduced or cut off artificial heat. I successfully grew Rhododendrons and Camellias in an unheated pantry when the nighttime temperatures dropped to 40 degrees. The plants flourished.

Having an indoor garden is a real pleasure—what is more warming than an orchid in flower on a gray winter day, or the colorful beauty of a geranium? In summer you have your outdoor garden for color, but in winter, when the world is blanketed in snow or darkened by dreary rain, the indoor greenery with its soothing color becomes a treasure indeed, one you can enjoy regardless of your indoor temperature.

♫ ♫ Good Selections

From my years in a Chicago apartment I found that the hairy-leaved Begonias and some rhizomatous varieties could withstand coolness if necessary and do quite well: indoors, some nights the thermometer was at 50°F. Once established and in large pots, these Begonias almost took care of themselves, and they produced numerous lovely bowers of small flowers in mid-winter. Today, twenty years later, I still have two Begonias from that collection, and they are growing beautifully in my plant room.

Geraniums have vibrantly colored flowers and handsome foliage and are available in many types, including the popular zonal and Martha Washington, but generally they are difficult to grow indoors. However, they *can* be grown, if you give them warmth during the day and coolness at night. With a lengthy period of adjustment and dedicated care they will often reward you by blooming and flourishing in your home.

You may believe that all cacti grow naturally only in the desert. That's not so. Many, including the popular Christmas cactus, grow in damp and cool rain forests. These types of cacti are what we're concerned with here. I treat most of my cacti and succulents as I do my epiphytic Orchids: I grow them in a mixture of equal parts of fir bark and soil and give them bright but not intense light. They thrive.

Among the cacti and succulents are some that do need warmth in the summer but must have coolness in the winter to complete their growing cycle. There are plenty of varieties of cacti and succulents just right for chilly locations.

For decades, orchids were considered to be greenhouse plants, most suitable for high humidity and heat. We now know how incorrect this concept was; most orchids prefer a very airy environment and rather cool temperature. (There are exceptions, of course. Some varieties of orchid do need heat but these are a minority.) Today, orchids are perhaps one of the most favorite of houseplants because they usually are easy to grow. Selection is the key to success with these plants and there are hundreds of different kinds you can grow in a cool house or apartment. And flowering plants that are more beautiful are indeed hard to find.

The South African bulbous plants naturally prefer cool nights (50°F), so here is a group of plants Mother Nature seemingly intended for chilly apartments and houses. And what fine plants! The flowers are exquisite, from the fine blue blooms of Agapanthus to the lovely white blossoms of *Eucharis grandiflora*. And don't ignore the exotic brilliant red blooms of the Vallota species. Bulbs from areas other than South Africa are also suitable candidates for the chilly house. Among these are the popular Narcissus and beautiful Gloxinias.

Bromeliads are a vast family of plants that have become very popular in the last decade. Basically, Bromeliads are vase- or tube-shaped and have scanty roots. Aechmeas, Billbergias, Guzmanias, Neoregelias, Nidulariums, Tillandsias, and Vrieseas are some of the many suitable members of this family. I grow these plants in my plant room at daytime temperatures of 70°F and nighttime temperatures of 50° to 55°F. In nature, Bromeliads grow on tree tops and rocks in areas where it is generally quite cool. Most Bromeliads are native to Mexico and South America, but they do not need extreme heat. Some are large plants (to 60 inches), but most are medium sized (to 30 inches), making them fine indoor subjects. Bromeliads are grown mainly for their beautiful foliage and ability to survive low light levels. If your rooms are partially heated by day and quite cool at night, Bromeliads are for you.

𝒮 𝒮 Other Cool Growers

We've not yet exhausted the list of plants you can grow in cool places. Ruellias are stellar performers, as are Impatiens (a bit difficult to get growing) and Azaleas, Camellias, and Rhododendrons. These last two groups are essentially outdoor plants, but they can be grown successfully indoors. Fuchsias also perform well indoors, *if* they are given a great deal of care. Nor should you ignore such foliage favorites as Dracaenas and Pandanus. The selection of foliage plants that tolerate cool temperatures is not vast; most leafy beauties do like warmth. But some of these can succeed. More about those at the end of the next chapter.

𝒮 𝒮 𝒮 𝒮

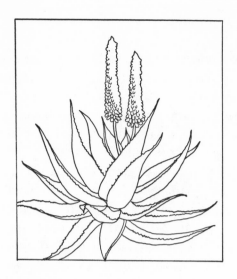

2

Some

Like It

Cool

As we've seen in Chapter 1, there are many plants that can be grown in cool places. However, when greenery is in cooler than normal conditions, culture of the plants is different from growing them in optimum circumstances.

With less heat, plants grow slowly and require less water. Feeding, too must be done with a careful hand. Light is still another factor, as is humidity. We will now look at these aspects in general (with more detailed instructions on specific plants in the next chapter).

♫ ♫ Water and Feeding

Water is still the most important part of successful indoor plant care (presuming light is good). Watering different plants can be tricky and although some folks mechanize their indoor gardens with gadgets to tell them when to water and how much, I believe this takes a great deal of pleasure out of gardening. (It is also costly.) Why bother with plants at all if you don't have the time to enjoy them.

How you water a plant is perhaps more vital than *when* you water. Apply water so all parts of the soil become moist—this means a thorough watering so that excess water drains from the holes in the bottom of the container. Include sufficient drainage materials—shards, stones, or broken pieces of brick. The many-sided surfaces of these materials help water evaporate and keep it from accumulating in the soil. Avoid waterlogging your soil.

Scanty watering creates pockets of dry soil causing roots to probe and push to seek moisture—this weakens a plant.

Use tepid water. The best way is to let it stand overnight in a bucket or can. Cold water shocks plants and if coupled with cool soil temperatures that can harm a plant. Maintain a watering schedule of twice or three times a week, depending upon the amount of artificial heat to which they've been subjected. The more heat, the more water you'll need because artificial heat dries out plants faster than you might imagine.

When you set up a watering schedule for your plants consider the following:

Size of pot—Small pots dry out faster than large ones.

Material of pot—Plastic holds water; clay pots facilitate evaporation of moisture.

Amount of light—If light is less than good, water less often than if light is bright.

Temperature—If temperatures are cool (50°F) water less often than when in the 60s or higher.

Variety of plant—Most plants like an evenly moist soil (throughout pot); there are exceptions, however, such as cacti which like a barely moist soil in winter.

Most gardeners feed plants sporadically throughout the year and if you have extra money, this may be well and good. However, excess feeding has severe drawbacks; too much can create toxic salts in the soil which can burn roots, and feeding in winter to try to force plants to grow (when most of them need to rest) can kill a plant.

If you must use plant food, use less—never more. Spring and summer are the best times to feed. Avoid applying additional food in fall and winter. Some plants—those that are in very large pots and are not repotted annually—do require feeding. But most plants in smaller pots, repotted in fresh soil yearly, need very little food.

♫ ♫ Repotting

Repotting a plant is necessary not only to allow the plant more room to grow but also because fresh soil provides the nutrients your plants need to prosper—no matter whether it is grown in coolness or warmth. And repotting a plant is not difficult. Do a few each week in early spring.

Plants in very small pots up to approximately 8 inches need repotting every nine months.

Plants in containers from about 8 inches up to 18 inches in diameter should be repotted every 12 to 18 months.

Plants in larger containers should be repotted every third year.

Repotting consists of taking a plant from its present container and putting it into fresh soil in a different, usually larger, pot. Knock the edge of the old pot against a table edge to loosen the rootball (put foil over the top of the soil so it does not fall out) or gently tap the pot sides with a hammer. Once the rootball is loose tease it out, and then crumble away the old soil and trim any brown roots. Shake the plant to loosen soil particles. Now take a clean pot, insert drainage materials, add a mound of new soil, center the plant, and fill in and around with fresh soil. Tap the bottom of the pot on a flat surface to settle the soil and then add more soil and press it into place with your thumbs. Water thoroughly. Then you may want to label the plant so you'll be sure to remember what you're growing.

POTTING WITH SOIL OR BARK

1- USE BROKEN POT PARTICLES OR SMALL PEBBLES FOR DRAINAGE MATERIAL.

2- ADD MOUND OF SOIL OR BARK.

3- CENTER PLANT ON MOUND. FILL WITH SOIL.

4 - PACK SOIL AROUND PLANT AND WATER.

♫ ♫ Light, Humidity, Air

All plants need light to grow and as a general rule the more light they receive the better they'll perform. In the cold months, however, natural light is not very plentiful in most regions; still, you needn't panic. Most plants can get along fine with only bright light—direct sun isn't necessary, and can harm some varieties. But if there is some sun so much the better.

Humidity has always been an important factor in growing healthy plants indoors—generally the amount of moisture in a room is low. But in cool conditions plants neither want nor need very much humidity—an average of 20 to 30 percent is usually fine. An inexpensive hygrometer placed in the growing area tells you how much moisture is in the air. You can buy this instrument at most hardware stores. Too much humidity coupled with cloudy days and coolness can create a breeding ground for fungus diseases. However, too little humidity (less than 20 percent) can dessicate your plants. You can always increase the amount of moisture your plants receive from the air by misting them once a day or so. Hairy-leaved plants and cacti are exceptions; they should never be misted.

Even in cool temperatures plants require good air circulation to grow well. This doesn't mean that you should open your windows and allow precious heat to escape. A small electric fan operating at low speeds helps to keep air moving. The Braun Manufacturing Company offers a 7-inch fan that works fine for small indoor garden areas. It uses little energy, too.

If the weather is not too cold by all means open a window a crack—not in the plant area but near it so that fresh air can circulate in the room. Few plants like stagnant conditions. Most want a light, airy atmosphere.

𝒮 𝒮 General Hints

Occasionally, insects and disease may attack plants in the home but you can reduce the incidence and severity of these attacks if you keep the growing area clean.

If light is very poor in the plant area, use a plant-growth lamp—new ones fit standard reading lamp sockets. For more details see the later chapter on artificial light.

Plants are free with offspring, so grow your own; you needn't spend money for new plants. I'll tell you how to do that in a later chapter.

And finally, always remember that plants are a responsibility. You must care for them and spend some time with them—they need attention just as a dog or cat does.

𝒮 𝒮 𝒮 𝒮

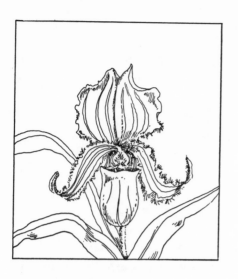

3

How and Where To Buy Plants

It will be difficult to select cool-growing plants at a local florist or plant shop. Most plants now have commercial growers' tags with instructions and invariably these read: "grow at 72° to 78°F." A statement like this is a dangerous generalization;however, it puts the plant seller in a safe position. But how do *you* determine the cool growers from the really tropical plants in this lump-a-bunch situation? (It is not always possible to travel with this book in your hand.)

First, let us look at the various places to buy plants and then later we can solve the important problem of the proper plants for cool places.

♫ ♫ Plant Stores, Florists

Neighborhood plant shops and florists may be a convenient place to purchase plants. However, in most cases, the selection is limited and specific advice on a particular species is usually not available (other than the tags I have mentioned). If you buy in these places, know what you want before you go, take a list with you, and ask for plants by botanical name.

Although most plant shops and florists have a limited stock (there is only so much space), many of these establishments will order a plant for you. Another advantage to local suppliers is that you can return a plant if it does not satisfy you—generally, most owners will honor this policy.

For the convenience and general return policy you will probably pay high prices at florists and plant shops. You yourself must decide if the price is worth the advantages of a local source.

♫ ♫ Mail Order Suppliers

The mail order company is my choice for purchasing plants; here you are privy to a catalog, can look at it at your leisure, and find what you want. Furthermore, many catalogs do list temperature preferences for plants, especially companies that specialize in Orchids, Begonias, and the other varieties mentioned earlier.

Prices at mail order suppliers are usually quite fair and if there is a problem with a plant you can write asking for information and advice. Reputable companies, whose sole business is plants, are very careful about proper botanical names which can be valuable information when you are trying to get care-help for a specific plant in gardening books.

Shipping from mail order companies goes on all year with the exception of the very hot or very cold months and there are various ways to get plants to you: parcel post, air freight, and so on. Air freight delivery is usually overnight but it is costly and based on the one-hundred pound rate. Even if you are ordering only one plant, you would pay the same as, say, for ten. Most plants can travel several days in closed boxes without harm. (There are, of course, exceptions and these mainly include very tropical plants that need excessive moisture.)

You will find ads for mail order companies in the classified sections of garden magazines. While there is usually a charge for a catalog, the price is often deductible from the first order.

With mail order purchase you can usually get the plant you want for the conditions you have—whether it be cool or cold. Peruse the catalog first, then write, if necessary, to verify your selections. Or match names and descriptions of plants from this book with lists of plants in the catalog.

𝄞 𝄞 When the Plants Arrive

Most companies ship plants bare root—that is, out of the pot and with little or no soil. It is far better for the health of the plant to pay the extra shipping cost and have the plants left in their containers, if this service is provided. If still potted, there is less shock to the plant as it gets accustomed to new conditions. When you receive your plants, don't put them in direct sun as soon as you have them out of the box—this could harm them. Instead, put the plants in a bright place where there is good air circulation. Leave them there for a few days before putting them in permanent positions at windows.

Repotting will be necessary with most of the new plants you get—some may be in soilless mediums, others may be in soil that probably has been depleted of nutrients and the containers may not be pleasing to you. So after a few weeks I generally repot the plants in fresh soil and new containers to be sure the plant prospers.

When you get your plants they may not look too healthy—after their traveling time—but don't panic. Most plants recover in a period of a week or so.

𝄞 𝄞 How To Tell A Healthy Plant

If you buy in person, are there ways of determining a healthy plant from a sick one? You bet there are.

Look for plants with firm leaves and a perky character. Drooping, wan leaves mean something could be awry with its culture.

Plants in caked soil should be avoided.

Plants with insects on them are to be obviously left at the nursery—not brought into your home so the insects can travel to your other plants. Inspect leaf axils and the undersides of the foliage where most pests hide.

Look for fresh new growth when buying your plants—this indicates plants are in good health and growing. Avoid any plant with dead or faded leaves, bent stems, or ungainly growth structure.

☊ ☊ ☊ ☊

4

Places for Plants, Containers

To enjoy the plants in your house or apartment, you need to select those that appeal to the eye, complement your decoration, and that *will grow* within your home's temperature. Then display them attractively. In this way the flowers and foliage at your windows will always be a pleasing sight.

I am not suggesting you turn your home into a plant store. It isn't necessary. But by judicious selection you can have a stunning indoor garden. In the vast world of cool plants there are hundreds for average home conditions: handsome geraniums, some cacti, delightful African violets, stunning Orchids that don't require rainforest humidity (there are many), exotic Bromeliads. There is also a world of bulbous plants—Allium, Eucharis, Eucomis, Vallota, and more. All can brighten dreary winter days.

So, evaluate your conditions, select plants accordingly, and place them strategically for year-long indoor beauty.

At the same time you are analyzing temperature, think also about light. Some plants, such as Orchids, do well in ordinary bright light, while most of the cacti, such as Parodias and Lobivias, really need good sun to prosper.

An added consideration should be size: it is wise to think about whether you should use large, medium, or small plants when making selections for a particular area.

19

♫ ♫ Where To Display

You can just place a specimen here or there and leave it at that, but this will hardly add up to a handsome indoor garden. Why not arrange several plants esthetically to create a focal point in the room? Or turn a windowsill into a miniature garden by taking advantage of some of the many hardware devices for shelves and hangers. For example, three shelves fastened across a window will accommodate about eighteen medium-sized plants and so create a colorful picture.

A floor installation is another possibility. Use galvanized planter bins (available from sheet-metal shops), cut to fit your particular area. Use a 2-inch deep pan with rolled edges to avoid cuts from sharp projections. Fill the bins with pea-sized gravel to within about one-half to one inch from the top and set the plants on the gravel not in it. Keep the gravel slightly moist so as to furnish humidity for your plants.

Suspending plants at windows is another way to provide color in the home. Use handsome hanging containers—four or five at a window. Suspend the containers at different levels—high, low, and in between—and in a staggered design. A straight line of plants is monotonous and also difficult to care for. At varying levels and in different positions there is more visual interest (and you can easily move among the plants to water them). The hangers come in a variety of materials such as hemp, cord, and yarn; decorated or plain. Choose hangers to complement your containers and plants. I suggest you avoid overly fancy or colorful ones which would detract from the plants.

Tray shelves on "pressure poles" that attach to ceilings and walls without hardware offer another way of gardening indoors. These space-saving suspension poles make an interesting vertical garden with easy care.

A tea table wheeled next to a window creates a pretty garden, and the table can be easily moved about as the light changes. Do protect the surface with a piece of glass or some tiles and set the plants themselves on saucers.

♫ ♫ How To Display

For most window displays, avoid large plants—they will look awkward and ungainly. Don't use too many plants—a crowded area will look like a jungle. Select your containers with care. The standard terra-cotta pot is a wise basic choice—it looks good in almost any surrounding, comes in many sizes, has some variety of shape, and lets moisture evaporate slowly from the walls—a plus for plants.

Decorative containers such as a group of china or tole cache pots or some Chinese jardinieres can also be used. A great many ornamental glazed containers and handsome porcelain ones are also available. But don't plant directly in these as most do not have drainage holes. Instead use standard clay pots and slip these into the decorative ones. More on containers below.

You can also put pots into attractive, inexpensive baskets which can be found at plant shops, or variety and gift stores. Do protect the bottom of the basket against moisture.

So, whether on window shelves, on trays attached to poles, in planter boxes, or on tables next to the light, your plants can create a cheerful atmosphere in any room. It is all a matter of choosing the right plants for the conditions you have, displaying them properly, and, of course, caring for them so they will thrive diligently.

♫ ♫ Containers and Plant Furniture

In recent years, suppliers have provided not only new plants, but also many kinds of new containers. Once clay pots were all that was available to the home gardener, but today any nursery has pots and tubs of all sizes and in dozens of different materials. For the discriminating plant hobbyist, selecting the proper container is almost as important as choosing the right plant.

Plants with dark leaves look more harmonious in a darker-colored container—a terra-cotta pot, for example; which is medium dark in value. In a white pot, the effect would be jarring to the eye. On the other hand, pale yellow-green plants would be fine in white or straw-colored pots because the color values blend.

The standard clay pot is still with us, but in new designs and sizes. There are also fine glazed pots, ceramic containers, wooden tubs and pots, plastic and metal ones, jardinieres, and so forth for plants. Some containers are very ornamental, with outside scroll-work or bas-relief designs. Be sure the design of the pot does not clash with the style of your room furnishings.

The clay pot is still one of the most functional housings for a plant: plants grow well in them because they are porous, and the natural clay color harmonizes both with the plant itself and with most indoor furnishings. These containers are available in a number of designs:

1. Venetian pots are barrel-shaped, with a band design pressed into the sides in a scored texture. They come 12 to 16 inches in diameter and are somewhat formal in appearance, so use them with discretion.

2. The simple and handsome Italian pot modifies the border to a tight-lipped detail. Some of these pots have rounded edges, others are beveled or rimless, in sizes from 12 to 14 inches (20–35 cm). These pots are decorative and blend well with contemporary settings.

3. Spanish pots are graceful, with outward sloping sides, flared lips, come in sizes from 8 to 20 inches (20-50 cm), and have heavier walls than conventional clay ones. They look good in period rooms.

4. Azalea or fern pots are squat, limited in size to 14 inches (35 cm), and generally fine for most rooms. They are a visual relief from the standard vase-shaped pot.

5. Cylindrical pots are new. These terra-cotta containers are indeed handsome—a departure from the traditional tapered designs. They look well in almost any situation and come in four sizes, the maximum available in most areas being 16 inches (40 cm) in diameter.

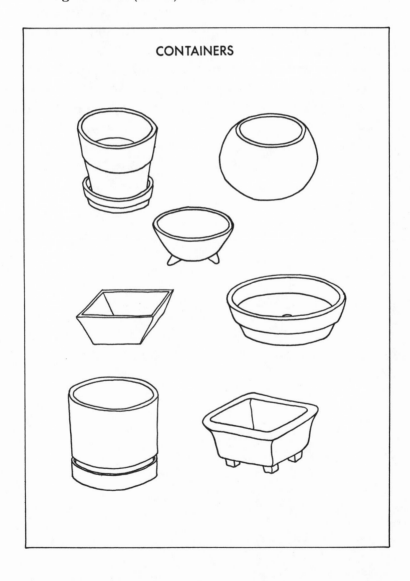

CONTAINERS

𝕏 𝕏 Other Containers

Although the unglazed pot is most popular, glazed containers have merit too. For example, they offer the buyer a variety of colors. But choose them carefully, because they can be overpowering, especially in large sizes. White is good for most interior color schemes, but some of the brighter colors may clash. Most glazed pots do not have drainage holes. Water plants in them moderately; overwatering will result in soggy soil that can kill plants. You can take them to a glass store in your area and have holes drilled. Or merely slip a potted plant into one of them and use the container simply as a "pot-hider."

Plastic pots may have a simple elegance, and three or four plants in plastic containers make an adequate decoration for a kitchen sill or a dining room sideboard. However, plastic pots have the great disadvantage that, because of their lightness, large plants have an alarming tendency to tip over in them.

𝕏 𝕏 𝕏 𝕏

5

Guide
to Growing
Cool Plants

Here is detailed guidance on just *how* to grow cool plants and what to expect from them. The plant groups covered here are not the only ones that thrive in chilly homes; they are the ones I can personally recommend from my own decades of experience. We'll start with flowering plants and end the chapter with some foliage beauties.

♫ ♫ Bromeliads

In nature, Bromeliads decorate landscapes, tree tops, and rocks, enjoying natural air currents, rainfall, humidity, and seasonal temperatures. A few grow in the ground like other houseplants. They are very adaptable and, in your home, Bromeliads will thrive at windows at any exposure. When they bloom, you can move them about for table decoration or corner accents (in my living room I had a *Neoregelia carolinae* that was colorful for three months).

Plastic trays, available in various sizes, are a great convenience for windowsills, and sheet-metal houses make galvanized metal trays that can also be fitted to window space. Fill the pan with crushed stone to within ½ inch of its top; set potted Bromeliads on top of the stone. Small Bromeliads are especially displayed this way.

Light

If your windows are obscured by tall buildings and thus need additional light, use fluorescent lighting tubes on ready-made stands or trays that accommodate ten to twenty plants and provide adequate "sunshine" for your plants' needs. Position the plants so the tops of their leaves are twelve to fifteen inches from the light tubes. Sun-loving species like *Ananas comosus* and *Hechtia rosea* need about sixteen hours of light; partial shade varieties need about thirteen hours. Use an automatic timer to control on and off periods. More detailed information on growing plants under light is at the end of the guide.

Watering and Feeding

I keep the "vase" of a Bromeliad filled with water through spring, summer, and fall. Since the leaves of Bromeliads are hard and durable, the weakest part of the plant is the core, the vase. If the vase holds water too long, and the water does not drain off naturally in the potting medium, a Bromeliad is apt to rot at this vulnerable point. Apply water vertically to the vase. In winter I let the vases dry out somewhat.

In any season, I find that some drying out of the soil between waterings is beneficial. In the summer and fall I water the plants about every third day. In the winter and spring I water every fourth or fifth day, depending upon whether the sun is bright or the sky is cloudy or rainy.

For Bromeliads, a shower in the sink once every two weeks is wise because it leaches out built-up acids from the soil. In areas of rainy summers you can set your Bromeliads outside on a porch; a few weeks of outdoor air and rain water will refresh plants noticeably.

Outdoors in nature, leaves and debris decompose in the vases and in turn provide nutrients essential to the plants' growth. Under indoor cultivation, Bromeliads require a weak compensating fertilizer. I use a 10-5-5 solution once every two weeks in the spring and summer but not through the rest of the year.

Air Circulation

In their natural state, Bromeliads are found mostly on the edges of rocks or cliffs, high in trees, or in the mountains, where the air is cool and moist. In other words, they grow where there is a free movement of air because this is vital to their health. This is the most important aspect to remember of home culture: Bromeliads will not thrive in a stuffy atmosphere—do not crowd them.

In the summer, and whenever weather permits in other seasons, I keep windows near the plants open, even through the night. In inclement weather, when the windows must be closed, I run a small fan near the plants to create a gentle flow of air. (This also discourages fungus disease and insects.) I carefully avoid drafts, however.

Since Bromeliad roots benefit from air as much as the leaves, I recommend planting Bromeliads in orchid pots that have slotted sides or in any other container that has side openings. It is also beneficial to hang the pots so air can circulate freely around them. You might try hanging pots with wires suspended from curtain rods, or use the wire baskets now available at most florists. Remember that the more air Bromeliads get, the better they grow.

Containers and Potting

Small containers are best for most species of Bromeliads. They protect plants from a stagnant, soggy soil, since small pots dry out faster than large ones. The standard orchid clay pot in the four-or five-inch size is good, even for larger specimens. For example, I have a *Billbergia zebrina* that is almost four feet high in a four-inch pot. This is top heavy, especially when the vase is filled with water, so I prop up the plant with slender bamboo stakes pushed deep into the soil at the edge of the pot. Then I loop string around the upper part of the plant and tie it to the stakes as an anchor. I do not use plastic pots because they are not heavy enough to support large Bromeliads. Hanging orchid baskets with openings between the slats are fine for pendant species like *Aechmea filicaulis* and some of the Billbergias.

Potting Bromeliads is relatively simple. Pot epiphytic and rock-growing Bromeliads in osmunda (tree fern fiber). Because this material is not a solid mass, it dries quickly and offers excellent drainage, which is vital to Bromeliads' growth. Orchid fir bark can also be used for these species. Terrestrial plants need a mixture of leaf mold, manure, and sand, with some crushed rock. Or, if you care to, experiment with a compost of your own, but ensure good drainage and aeration of the plants' roots. If you pot Bromeliads too tightly, water will not drain off and rot will develop at plants' bases.

Use cleaned pots and pot shards. I fill the pots one-third full with small stones or pot shards (just a few pieces). After soaking the osmunda overnight, then I work the osmunda to the center of the pot, firming it with my thumbs or a blunt stick. Do not set the base of the plant so deep that you crush the lower part of the leaf cup. Bromeliads that do not have much root system are difficult to handle, but they can be propped up with my stake method until roots develop. Many Bromeliads can be grown successfully on pieces of tree fern or orchid slabs. As you pot the plants, trim off any excess osmunda with scissors.

Insects

Bromeliads are amazingly free of trouble, seemingly never getting attacked by mealybugs, red spiders, or any other kind of insect, perhaps because the leaves are just too tough. However, Aechmea scale is an occasional enemy. These small (pinhead size) black, hard-shelled insects with sucking appendanges attach themselves to Bromeliads' leaves, usually on the undersides. Scrape off scale with the dull edge of a knife, and try not to bruise the foliage as you work. Soap and water and a stiff brush may get rid of scale, too, if the attack is not advanced. Their shell is impervious to most insecticides and anyway, Bromeliads react poorly to insecticides. If absolutely necessary, use a very mild solution of Malathion.

Bromeliad Selections

Here are the Bromeliads I grow that do very well in cool conditions:

Billbergia nutans

Billbergia nutans (queen's tears)
A large plant to 48 inches with grassy, dark green leaves. Flower spikes appear on short stems from the base of the cups of rosette growth. Flowers are pendent. Colors of chartreuse and cerise and pink predominate. Flowers last a short time but are exotic. Easy to grow: immune to cold.

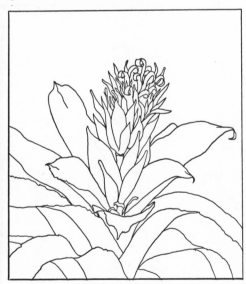

Billbergia pyramidalis

Billbergia pyramidalis
Another fine tubular-shaped Bromeliad with dark gray-green leaves and handsome flower bracts of bright pink; bracts are very colorful; flowers small and insignificant.

Guzmania lingulata

Guzmania lingulata

An apple green, leaved rosette to 20 inches with a flower crown of orange-red bracts or white that lasts for months. Not to be missed. Does well in coolness.

Guzmania monostachia

Guzmania monostachia (red hot poker plant)

This Bromeliad has dark green leaves and produces a most unusual inflorescence of brown, white, and red in a poker style. Lasts a long time. Excellent for the home.

Neoregelia carolinae

Neoregelia carolinae 'Tricolor'

This 40-inch, rosette Bromeliad has become a favorite with indoor gardeners. It has variegated green-yellow and pink foliage—very beautiful. Small flowers appear in cup of plant at bloom time and leaves are flushed with red.

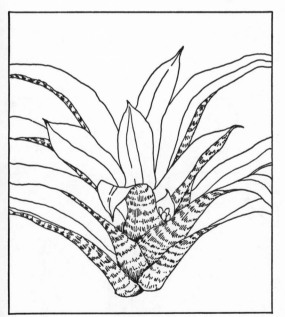

Neoregelia spectabilis

Neoregelia spectabilis (fingernail plant)

Another rosette Bromeliad, to 30 inches, with dark green leaves tipped with red. Center of plant turns fiery red at bloom time and small pink flowers hide in cup of plant. Very pretty and sure to bloom.

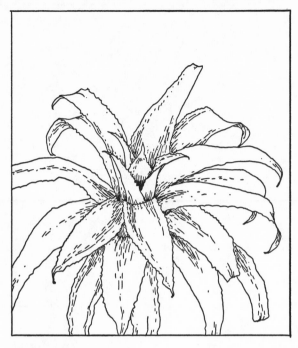

Nidularium fulgens

Nidularium fulgens

A 20-inch rosette Bromeliad, quite pretty with mottled leaves and tiny violet flowers. Center of plant turns pink or red at bloom time.

Nidularium innocentii

Nidularium innocentii

A handsome 30-inch rosette type plant with dark gray green leaves, white flowers, and center of plant flushes red at bloom time.

Tillandsia cyanea

Tillandsia cyanea

An unusual Bromeliad to 20 inches, with grassy dark green leaves. Two-inch purple flowers on the pinkish red spike appear like butterflies perched on leaves. Very unusual, handsome, and sure to please.

Tillandsia ionanthe

Tillandsia ionanthe

A tiny 2- to 3-inch plant with tufted leaves; center of plant turns bright red at bloom time and tiny purple flowers accompany this colorful harvest. Easy to grow on cork slabs, bark, or even just pinned to a curtain. Unique.

Vriesea hieroglyphica

Vriesea hieroglyphica

A large, 40-inch rosette plant with exquisite foliage—green accented with purple and banded with darker colors. A superior foliage plant.

Vriesea splendens

Vriesea splendens (flaming sword)

A popular Bromeliad with apple green rosette of leaves and an erect spike of yellow and orange or fiery red, with yellow flower bracts looking like a flaming sword. Grows easily.

♫ ♫ Cacti and Succulents

Light

Succulents and cacti need all the light they can get to grow into beautiful specimens, although when in a shaded situation, such as a dark dry corner, the plants will survive—they just will not grow well and prosper—I know this from experience. If you want flowers, the plants definitely must have some sun during the day. So for plants' maximum health, put them near windows. In the spring, fall, and winter succulents and cacti can take as much direct sun as possible. But in the summer shield the plants from the strong, direct sun rays by using curtains, venetian blinds, or rollups.

Light at an east or south window is the best because it is bright and provides a few hours of sun. North exposures are always a problem, but some succulents and cacti, such as waxplants, sansevieria, Christmas cactus, and rhipsalis, will grow under north light. In good weather put plants as close as possible to the window, but in the winter move them back so they will not get chilled.

Plants that are not near windows should face the light. Light in the center of a room is generally poor, so if you must grow plants there, occasionally move them to window areas so they can regain their strength.

Temperature and Air Circulation

Average fall, winter, and spring home temperatures of 75°F by day and 65°F at night suit most succulents and cacti; higher summer temperatures will not harm them. Most cacti and succulents need a rest in the winter, so cool conditions suit them fine (50° to 55°F at night).

Plants must have a good circulation of air to thwart fungus diseases, which proliferate in stagnant conditions, and to contribute to the overall health of your plants. Most of the year leave the window open slightly, being careful not to let your cacti and succulents sit in a direct draft from windows, heating units, or cooling ducts. Drafts can almost kill cacti and succulents. In winter, keep a small fan on at low speed to help air circulate if you cannot leave the windows open.

Watering and Feeding

Most people water their houseplants too much or too little, but succulents and cacti can adjust either way, as long as they get *some* water. To set up a schedule, first consider the size of the container. Plants in small containers—three to four inches—need more frequent watering than plants in ten-inch pots because the soil in small pots dries out faster. A second consideration is the material of which the container is made: because clay is porous, soil in clay pots dries out quicker than soil in plastic or glazed containers. Also consider light and temperature conditions: do not water on cool, cloudy days because without enough light, plants cannot assimilate moisture properly.

There is no need to fertilize. Enough nutrients are in the soil to take care of their needs.

Soil and Potting

Although many cacti and succulents are native to sandy desert areas, they need a good soil mix indoors. The two- or three-pound packages contain enough soil for three or four six-inch containers; the three-cubic-foot bags provide enough soil for several plants in very large containers. The larger bag is always the most economical; if you do not need all that soil immediately, store the excess in a cool, dry place in an airtight container. If you have storage room, you can also buy bulk soil, which is the best because it is what nurseries use.

Packaged soils are sold under various trade names and in a variety of mixes, such as houseplant, African violet, or cactus soil. Squeeze the bag to determine if a package contains porous soil—so air and water can go through it—the package should feel crumbly.

I usually buy a packaged cactus soil mix and add two cups of sand to the hobby sack. (If I have some houseplant soil on hand, I add some sand to it. You can buy sand in packages at nurseries.) I also add some charcoal chips to the cactus soil because they keep the soil sweet and increase its porosity. Do not use the synthetic soilless mixes because they have few nutrients (in such mixes plants must be fed every watering).

The potting medium called fir bark (used for potting Orchids) is excellent for epiphytic succulents and cacti. Fir bark is also good for the jungle-type succulents and cacti, such as Christmas cactus; add one cup of fir bark to a six-inch pot of standard cactus soil.

Before you start to repot, make sure all the containers are clean, have drainage holes, and that the soil is dry. To handle any cacti and succulents with spines, wear gloves, or encircle plants with strips of folded newspaper.

Remove plants from small containers by first rapping the edges of the pots against a table or wooden shelf to loosen the plants. Never pull or grab plants from soil. Next, put on gloves or drape a heavy cloth or wadded newspaper over the plants and wiggle them. The idea is to gently tease the plants from their pots. Small plants should come out easily.

To remove medium-sized plants, tap the bases of the pots against a solid surface to loosen the plants. Do this several times with plants in five- or six-inch pots. If you still have trouble removing the plants, insert a wooden, blunt-nosed stick between the soil and the edges of the pots. Poke the stick in and out of each pot, around the diameter of the soil line. Then, with gloves on, grab the top of the plant and gently tease it from the old soil.

Large plants are almost impossible to take out of pots because of their weight, so first hit the sides of the containers with a rubber mallet. Then use the potting stick and try to lift the plants out of their old soil. If the plants have been in their pots for several years, these methods may not extricate the plants, so you should go ahead and break the pots with a hammer. This is *not* foolish; it is better to destroy pots than plants, and I guarantee that playing tug-of-war with plants will destroy them. (Use the broken pieces of the pot as drainage-hole covers.)

Once your plants are out of their old soil, crumble away all the old soil from the roots. Do this gently by combing your fingers through the soil. If you notice any dead (brown) roots, judiciously cut them off, but never cut more than you must. Leave the rootball intact.

Now prepare the new containers: put some broken pieces of clay pots over the drainage holes, and add a mound of soil to each pot. Put the plants on the soil and center them; if they look too high, take out some soil; if they look too low, add some. Fill in and around the plants with soil, adding enough until the soil level is one or two inches from the tops of the pots. Tap the pots on a solid surface to settle the soil. Next, with your thumb or a blunt-edged stick, press down the soil to eliminate any air pockets—you want it to be firm but not tightly packed.

If the plant is spiny and thus apt to hurt your hand, put the soil in a newspaper chute or kitchen funnel and funnel it around the plant. Rap the bottom of the pot on a table to settle the loose soil and then add more soil. Finish by pressing the soil in place with a long wooden stick.

Cacti and Succulent Plants

Here are some cool growing cacti and succulents for your indoor garden:

Agave victoriae-reginae

Agave victoriae-reginae

If I were asked to name the most beautiful foliage plant, I think I would select this 14-inch rosette-type succulent. Leaves are dark green and penciled at the edges with white tracery—a very handsome plant.

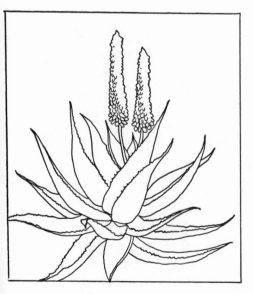

Aloe ferox

Aloe ferox

A common Aloe, this succulent to 20 inches has dark green leathery leaves in a rosette growth and fine bright orange-red flowers. Not spectacular but a very dependable plant.

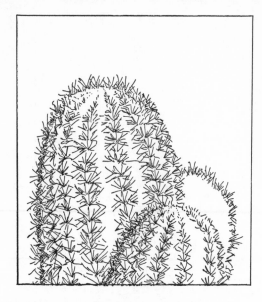

Echinocactus grusoni

Echinocactus grusoni (barrel cactus)

I have always been fond of this 24-inch green globe covered with yellow spines. It is a handsome plant and one that grows well indoors in almost any conditions. Don't expect flowers—I have had mine 12 years and have yet to see a bloom.

Euphorbia pulcherrima

Euphorbia pulcherrima *(*poinsettia)

The popular Christmas plant, to 36 inches, has leafy green leaves and is branching. It is the leaf bracts turning red at the seasonal time that has made it the desirable Christmas symbol. Plants are easy to grow in cool conditions and can be carried over year to year if you can cut them back in spring and set them in the garden.

Hoya carnosa (waxplant)

This popular succulent is a trailer, to 40 inches, and has oval leathery leaves. Bears clusters of waxy, pinkish white flowers, heavily scented. Not the easiest plant to grow but does like cool places.

Kalanchoe blossfeldiana   **Kalanchoe uniflora**

 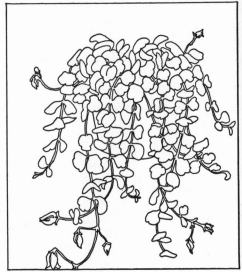

Kalanchoe
   Many of these now available; the most popular is *K. blossfeldi-ana* with small dark green leaves and masses of brilliant red flowers. Very pretty. *K. uniflora*, somewhat less attractive, has pink to orange bell flowers, small, trailing leaves. Unusual.

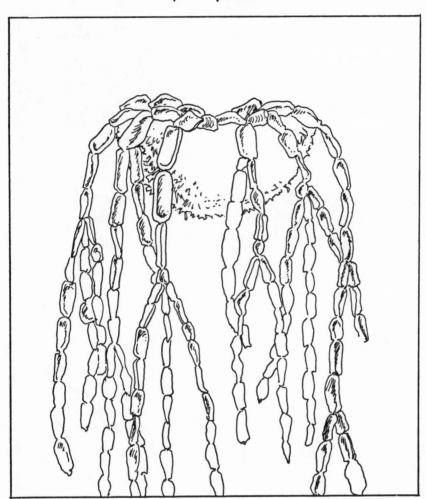

Rhipsalis paradoxa (mistletoe cactus)

Another trailing plant, to 10 inches, this cactus has pencillike leaves and bears small white flowers followed by berries. It is prized more for its bizarre appearance than its beauty but is different and desirable in the garden.

Rochea coccinea

Rochea coccinea

A most unusual 1-2 foot high succulent and a good one; handsome small leaves and fiery red flowers make it a very desirable plant. Somewhat tough to grow but likes cool places.

Zygocactus truncatus

Zygocactus truncatus

Whether you call this Christmas cactus or Easter cactus, here is an amenable plant with dark green, leathery, clawlike stems (actually the leaves) and pretty pink or cerise flowers at tip ends, many to a plant. These cacti—and there are so many varieties—are really superior houseplants and can tolerate very cold conditions. Highly recommended.

ℐ ℐ Orchids

This large group of plants belong to the Orchidaceae family. Contrary to popular opinion, orchids are not parasites, although many are air plants (epiphytes). In nature, they mainly grow lodged on trees or bushes but derive no direct nourishment from the hosts. It is the minerals in rain water that help keep orchids alive; the plants use trees and bushes only for footholds. There are also botanical orchids that grow in soil. These are called *terrestrials.*

Temperature and Air Circulation

Cool-growing genera of Odontoglossum, Masdevallias, and some Miltonias need nights of 50°F; without this temperature they fail to bloom—they are excellent plants for chilly places. I find that circulation of air is more important for successful growing of orchids than almost any other factor since most orchids are air plants. I run two small electric fans at low speed in hot weather (directed away from the plants) to provide a gentle movement of air in the growing area. In winter, I keep one fan on to keep air moving. I shut off the fans at night unless the room seems stuffy.

Orchids respond poorly to sudden changes of temperature and to drafts, so when you ventilate, open windows other than those beside the plants; you can thus freshen the atmosphere indirectly.

Watering and Humidity

If your winter temperature fluctuates, so must your home-watering schedule. The more that artificial heat dries out the air, the more water orchids will need. The sizes of the pots also affect watering because small pots dry out faster than large pots. The type of compost is also a factor: fir bark dries out faster than osmunda. If a pot feels light when you pick it up, it generally means the compost is dry and should be watered. If the pot feels heavy in your hand, wait to water. Some growers put a thin layer of sphagnum or peat moss over the surface of the potting material. When this dries out, they water. If you are in doubt, do not water. It is important to use tepid water of about 60 to 70°F; no plant likes to be shocked with ice cold water.

High humidity is not necessary for orchids: 30 to 40 percent is fine. Orchids do better with lower humidity, along with a lower temperature at night. Some species do need high humidity, but these are the exceptions. Humidity will vary depending on where you live, but there are ways to increase or reduce it artificially.

If you are using galvanized trays with gravel or gravel-filled saucers, a certain amount of humidity will be provided by the evaporation of the excess water draining from the plants. Misting the air around the plants will increase humidity for a few hours, and the old-fashioned method of pans of water on radiators has its uses. Daily misting or spraying is necessary on sunny days in spring and summer. In autumn and winter, this is only necessary, say, once a week.

Potting Materials

Many potting materials have been used for orchids. Osmunda fiber has proved satisfactory through the years, although fir bark is now very popular. Pumice stone and charcoal can also be used. I cannot recommend an ideal compost: I don't think one has been found yet. Each kind has advantages as well as disadvantages. I pot many orchids in the bark of the Douglas white fir tree that has been graded into chunks of varying size and then steamed. Prepared bark is available in small, medium, and large pieces—all sizes are suitable. If you use fir bark, be sure to sift out any particles that are sometimes mixed in during the processing, because the particles may prevent drainage.

Osmunda fiber, or osmundine, is the fibrous aerial root of two types of osmunda fern. Although more difficult to pot with than fir bark, it does have advantages. This fiber holds water, dries out slowly over a long period, and has space between the fibers to permit circulation of air. As the material decays, usually in two to three years, it releases mineral nutrients vital for growth.

Potting

All potting materials must be absolutely clean. Wash and scrub pots and broken pieces of pot in scalding water. When you remove a plant from a pot, try not to force or pull it out because pressure can damage live roots. As mentioned in previous sections, gently tap the outside of the pot with a hammer and gradually tease the plant out of the old pot. Then carefully clean away all old compost from around the roots, and cut off any shriveled dead roots.

Fill the new pot one-third to one-half full with broken pieces of pot. Set the plant into the pot, then fill (to within half an inch of the rim) with fresh bark or other compost, occasionally pressing it down with a blunt-edged potting stick or piece of wood. Always work from the sides of the pot to the center. Stake the plant, if necessary, with wire or wooden sticks. Most orchids require tight and hard potting; a few are better loosely planted. Some growers recommend the use of wet bark, that is, bark first soaked overnight. But I use dry bark and it proves satisfactory.

When you are potting with fir bark, make sure the drainage is good; excess moisture at the root ball means disaster. In fact, more orchids are killed by overwatering than by any other error of culture, but if they had been potted properly, the good drainage would compensate.

Feeding

Fir bark is deficient in nitrogen, so you must supplement with fertilizer. A 20–10–10 or a 10–5–5 formula (figures indicate percentages of nitrogen, phosphoric acid, and potash) is excellent. The contents are plainly marked on the bottle. When an orchid is in active growth, apply the fertilizer about every ten to fourteen days. The time of growth varies with the individual species; for some plants, it will be spring and summer, others, autumn and winter.

Many species react adversely to heavy feeding, so fertilize with care. Too much nitrogen can prevent flowering. You may have to try different brands of fertilizers to check reactions under your conditions. Once every month, in winter too, apply a weak solution of Atlas Fish Emulsion.

Plants in osmunda require little if any additional feeding. If they are in active growth, about once every five weeks is enough, and none at all during autumn and winter.

Promoting Bloom

Keep a careful eye on your orchids for poor growth. If the leaves of a plant start to turn yellow, check the amount of water you are giving (it could be too much), and the possibility of too much sun. If the compost or bark stays soggy, stop watering altogether. Then, if it is still moist after seven or eight days, remove the plant from the pot. I do not immediately repot. Instead, I wrap the plant loosely in newspaper and put it in a cooler place, about 60°F, where there is good air circulation. In a day or two, I pot it again as usual. If a plant falls from a stand or window tray, do not throw it away. Trim the bruised or cracked areas with a sterilized knife (I use a sharp pocketknife) and repot.

To the eye, an orchid may appear completely dormant for months of the year—no root activity, no green growth, nothing in evidence. Do not try to force growth under these conditions. When the plant is ready to grow, you will see the signs—a fresh white root or a tiny green shoot.

When a plant refuses to bloom even though it has had proper culture, it may need a different day length. If you have fluorescent lights, you can experiment with different amounts of light and the plant may bloom. Otherwise, hope for the best; it is not possible to be 100 percent successful getting orchids to flower. Even light reflected from across the street or quite far away can have an effect. I had a Cattleya species that did not bloom for two years, not even a hint of a bud. I moved it to the floor away from the glare of the street lamps at night and it blossomed the same year.

If you plan to cut the flowers, let them stay on a plant for two to three days before you cut them. It takes this long for color and form to develop fully. When you cut, use a sterilized knife. I run a match flame over the blade for a few seconds. The heat also seals the cut stem.

Sometimes a plant fails to respond even under the best culture. I believe this is because it is a weak specimen that cannot adjust to the necessary change of environment. If I have space, I keep it; otherwise, out it goes.

Orchid Favorites

The following are some of my favorite cool-growing orchids:

Coelogyne cristata

Coelogyne cristata

One of the most desirable members of the orchid family. It has tapered, dark green leaves, grows to 24 inches and bears 2-inch exquisite white flowers with crystalline texture, dotted bright yellow in center of lip. An absolute beauty that likes it very cool (45°F).

Coelogyne massangeana

Coelogyne massangeana

A 40-inch plant with lovely broad green leaves—handsome even without bloom. Flowers, borne on pendent scapes (leafless flower stalks) from the base of the bulbs, are beige and brown, about one-half inch across, and last for several weeks. Very easy to grow.

Cymbidium 'Pixie'

Cymbidium 'Pixie'

One of the smaller cymbidiums (growing to 36 inches) with grassy green leaves. Flower spikes appear from base of bulb and bear dozens of 1- to 2-inch blooms, usually pink but there may be color variations.

Lycaste aromatica

Lycaste aromatica (cinnamon orchid)

This 24-inch plant has broad, green ribbed leaves and bears handsome flowers on erect stems; many to a plant after foliage fades. Flowers are butter-yellow and cinnamon scented. A fine small plant for limited space.

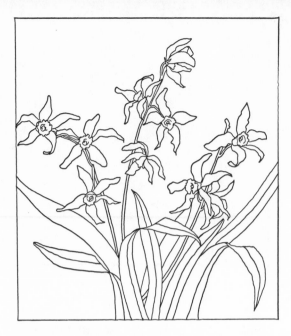

Miltonia candida

Miltonia candida (pansy orchid)

A cool-growing orchid that has chestnut brown flowers tipped with yellow. Not spectacular but attractive and sure to bloom.

Miltonia roezlii

Miltonia roezlii

Very pretty orchid growing to 20 inches, with large white flowers, lip scalloped and stained yellow splashed with red. Plants bear several flowers. Easy to grow.

Odontoglossum citrosmum

Odontoglossum citrosmum

A lovely, white, flowering orchid with dark green leaves. Plants grow to 25 inches and bear flowers easily if in cold conditions—about 50°F.

Odontoglossum pulchellum

Odontoglossum pulchellum (Lily-of-the-Valley orchid)

One of the small Odontoglossums with compact growth to 14 inches and sprays of tiny white scented flowers, many to a stem. Very easy to grow and likes it cold.

Odontoglossum uro skinneri

Odontoglossum uro skinneri

A rather large plant (to 40 inches) with broad green leaves and long stems carrying 2-inch magenta and brown flowers. Very unusual and colorful. Sure to please.

Oncidium ornithorhynchum

Oncidium ornithorhynchum (butterfly orchid)

To 20 inches, this leafy orchid has delicate wands of tiny, lilac-colored flowers, as many as a hundred to a small plant. Can take very cold conditions and still thrive.

Paphiopedilum callosum

Paphiopedilum callosum (Balinese dancer)

Somewhat small, to 20 inches, this fine orchid has dark green, mottled leaves and lovely lady-slipper flowers, about 4 inches across; they are purple and green—very unusual and striking. Lasts for many weeks. Likes it cold.

Paphiopedilum fairieanum

Paphiopedilum fairieanum

One of the old-time favorites with straplike green leaves; grows to 30 inches and bears solitary, lacquerlike, and multicolored flowers on short erect stems. sure to bloom and an excellent cool-loving plant.

Paphiopedilum spicerianum

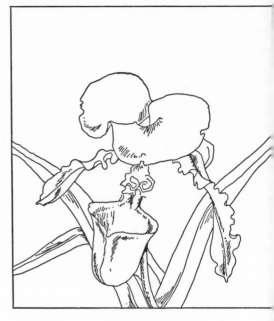

Paphiopedilum spicerianum

A fine lady-slipper orchid to 24 inches, with starlike leaves and handsome, multicolored 3-inch flowers on erect stems. Very pretty.

Zygopetalum crinitum

Zygopetalum crinitum

Not often seen but certainly deserving space in any indoor garden, this orchid has pseudobulbs and single, green leaves. Flowers are very handsome—about 1 inch across—with brown sepals and a large white lip laced with lavender.

Zygopetalum mackayi

A favorite plant growing to 30 inches, with large green leaves and solitary pseudobulbs. Flowers are large and vibrantly colored; predominately a blue hue. Very pretty.

♫ ♫ Begonias

Begonias are mainly from Brazil, Mexico, and Africa. Although they are fairly easy to grow, they still need care.

Light

Begonias are often considered shade plants, but this does not mean that they will grow and bloom in a dim hallway. In fact, many Begonias want all possible sunshine at south windows, especially in the winter. Others want bright light, and some need semishade. In the summer, some protection against the noonday sun is necessary; a window screen usually suffices.

Try to turn your plants once a week so that all the leaves get equal light and growth is uniform. For maximum growth keep them near windows where light is bright. Paint your room off-white to reflect more light (dark walls absorb light).

Soil

A good potting mix is a head start for successful Begonia growing. Begonias need a soil with nitrogen for good leaf growth, phosphoric acid for root development, and potash for strength. A good soil mix also contains iron, manganese, calcium, and other elements, and a sprinkling of bonemeal can always be added to promote flower production.

There are many recipes for a potting soil for Begonias. The type of mix to use depends on how you grow your plants and where you live. Begonias will grow in any soil—good, bad, or indifferent—for a length of time, but they will not prosper and become specimen plants. To do well, they must have the right kind of soil, with adequate nutrients. For many years I bought soil by the bushel from a local nursery; my plants grew reasonably well, but they did not really thrive. I started mixing my own soil for Begonias, and now I used packaged soil, prepared specifically for Begonias.

Watering and Feeding

Overwatering kills Begonias. If all other cultural conditions are good—soil, potting, light—a thorough soaking, followed by a drying out period before watering the soil again, is the best procedure. The roots have time to absorb all the moisture, and if they are somewhat dry for a day, there is little harm done. When to water depends on the weather, pot sizes, and individual location. You need to water specimen Begonias in ten- and twelve-inch pots once a week in winter, twice a week in early spring, and three times a week in summer. In the fall, go back to the twice-a-week schedule. Begonias in four- to six-inch pots need more care: In summer, water them daily. The rest of the year, water about three times a week, unless there is an unusually gray period (then once a week).

Some of the old-fashioned methods of determining when a plant needs water are still good. Feel the soil; if it is dry and crumbly, water. Lift the pot; dry ones weigh less than moist ones. Tap the side of a clay pot; if it has a hollow ring, water the plant.

When you water Begonias, really wet the soil until it becomes uniformly moist; this causes the roots to reach out and grow. Root development is hampered if only one section of the soil is moistened. If partial watering continues, roots in the dry areas stop growing and the plant dies.

Do not apply cold water because it shocks plants. I let a pail of water stand overnight for use in the morning. One-gallon plastic milk bottles are also useful for aging water. I try to water my plants, in the early morning hours rather than at night, when respiration is slow. Tap water is usually all right because it rarely contains minerals harmful to Begonias, but avoid artifically softened water since it is harmful to plants

Indoors, potted Begonias require feeding because repeated watering washes away nutrients. Fertilizer properly given is beneficial, producing healthy Begonias with strong leaf color and fine bloom. Administered recklessly, fertilizer is harmful if not fatal. Too much plant food locks the elements in the soil—it acts like a roadblock—and, ironically, the plant starves in the midst of plenty. Moderation is the rule. I use a 10-10-5 commercial soluble fertilizer, applying half the recommended dosage on the package label.

Fertilize plants when they are actively growing, usually in the spring and summer. In cold weather, when some Begonias are dormant, feed them only about every six weeks. Use Atlas Fish Emulsion in the summer, once every two weeks, but not all the rest of the year. If possible, every month flood your Begonias with a strong hose spray to leach out chemicals that have accumulated in the soil. This is important and should be done religiously.

Do not feed freshly potted Begonias because there are enough nutrients in new soil to sustain the plants for some time. Also do not feed ailing plants—the roots are not ready to absorb the nutrients. Treat for the problem first. Although foliar feeding—applying food to the leaves with a spray—is widely practiced, I have not found it satisfactory for Begonias. Too many rex and hirsute types resent lingering moisture on leaves.

Repotting

To repot plants, put small pieces of broken pots over the drainage hole of a clean container; add a few chunks of charcoal to keep the soil sweet. Fill the bottom of the pot with enough soil for a footing, place the plant in the center of the pot, and pour soil in and around the roots. Shake the container occasionally to settle the soil, and fill the pot to within a half inch of the rim. Do not pot a Begonia too firmly. Water the soil thoroughly, and place the plant in a warm, semishaded spot for a few days. Feed only when the plant starts to show new growth.

I do not follow a schedule for repotting. As a rule, spring is the best time because warm weather is on the way, but, when convenient, I have planted in the summer and fall without harming the plants. My system is simple: when roots grow through the drainage hole, the soil looks soggy, or a plant is neither growing nor dying, I repot it.

To remove a mature Begonia from a container, turn the pot upside down, hold the stem of the plant between your fingers with the tips of your fingers against the top of the soil, and tap the pot rim with a hammer. Gently tease the plant loose and remove the old soil from the roots. When repotting rhizomatous Begonias, do not cover the creeping rhizome with soil or rot will form. Let the rhizome remain on top of the soil, with the growing tip away from the pot's side.

In the winter many Begonias rest. When a healthy plant slows up and drops leaves, do not panic. Let the Begonia rest; water lightly, and omit fertilizer. Chances are the plant will spring to life at the first sign of warm weather. Rex Begonias are famous for this behavior; do not let them fool you, and do not try to force them to grow. A period of rest is natural in the life cycle of many plants.

Insects

Begonias are sometimes bothered by insects, but preventative measures go a long way in keeping plants free of pests and disease. Keep the growing area clean to help keep your Begonias healthy. Get rid of rotted leaves and flowers, and always work with clean tools and pots. When you buy Begonias from a grower you do not know, inspect them carefully, and then isolate the plants for about a week in an unheated place until you are sure they are pest-free.

If you grow many plants and insects are present, spray their area with an all-purpose insecticide—I use Malathion—every month when necessary. Isolate any suspected plants—those with limp growth or any that appear sickly. Do not crowd plants. Give each one ample room so air can circulate around it. If a few plants are attacked by insects, try spraying them heavily with water or dunking each plant in a bucket of water. But if the infestation is heavy, use an insecticide.

Begonia Selections

The following group of Begonias should be at home in cool temperatures:

Begonia alleryi

Begonia alleryi

Here is an old-time favorite, growing to 24 inches, with frosted green leaves accented with purple. The pale pink flowers appearing in clusters are handsome. Pinch out young leaves for well-shaped plants. Very nice.

Begonia 'Crestabruchii'

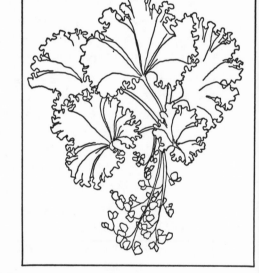

Begonia 'Crestabruchii' (lettuce begonia)

This is a very handsome Begonia with large yellow-green leaves, heavily ruffled and with twisted edges. The plant produces pink flowers. Will succeed with winter coolness. Different and desirable.

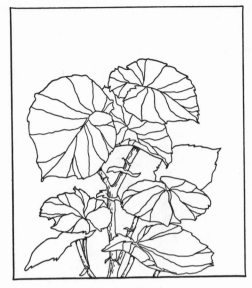

Begonia drostii

Begonia drostii

This is somewhat large (to 30 inches), with hairy, round dark green leaves and large red-bearded flowers. Can tolerate very cool conditions. A favorite of mine.

Begonia erythrophylla

Begonia erythrophylla (beefsteak begonia)

This has round leaves—green on top and red on the bottom. The 24-inch plant grows well in coolness and shade and produces fine pink flowers. Can tolerate almost any condition and grows fast.

Begonia luxurians

Begonia luxurians

This somewhat unusual Begonia (to 24 inches) has gray-green palmlike leaves and looks like a small tree. Although it is generally listed as a warm plant I have found mine does fine at 60°F at night.

Begonia 'Maphil'

Begonia 'Maphil' (Cleopatra begonia)

This is a fine example of nature at her best. The plant is 30 inches across and has exquisite leaves: gold, brown, and chartreuse. Plant bears tall spikes of tiny pink flowers. Highly recommended.

Begonia scharffiana

Begonia scharffiana

This is a robust, hairy plant with large olive green leaves and bountiful clusters of pink and white blooms. Very pretty and easy to grow.

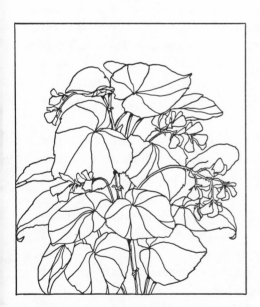

Begonia 'Viaudi'

Begonia 'Viaude'

A Begonia to 24 inches, this plant has cupped, olive green leaves and bearded white flowers. A compact plant that grows well with little care.

♪ ♪ Geraniums

Geraniums provide a wealth of beauty and color for the cool garden. Most of these plants thrive at nighttime temperatures of 45°F, if all other conditions are right. And there are almost thousands of varieties to choose from: standard types or zonals with scalloped leaves and brilliant single and double flowers, fancy-leaved types for the connoisseur, pretty dwarf growers, ivy-leaved types, and the popular Martha Washington varieties that thrive in cold places. With such a large family of plants it is difficult to suggest specific ways to grow each group, but the general cultural hints here should work well for most plants.

Soil and Watering

Geraniums do require somewhat more care than Bromeliads or even Orchids; however, the great plus with geraniums is that so many varieties bloom so abundantly and over so long a time.

Geraniums need a firm potting soil mixture. Add one part sand to packaged hobby-pack soil, and then toss in about a cupful of peat moss to provide the acid soil most geraniums like. Use small clay containers for geraniums—in large pots they do not grow as well as they prefer to have their roots crowded. Plants bloom best when potbound, so repot only when absolutely necessary, about every second year. If you want to add fresh soil, carefully dig out the top three to four inches of old soil and replenish with new. Always be sure drainage is perfect—excess water should pour from the bottom of the pot, and plants should never be in stagnant, water-soaked soil.

The Martha Washington and ivy-leaved geraniums rest somewhat in winter, so at that time water them only moderately—try to keep the soil just moist to the touch—and do not feed in winter. Watering is somewhat tricky with geraniums because they like moisture but resent any overwatering. Water thoroughly and then let the soil dry out somewhat. The amount of water required will vary with the size of the pot and the weather itself—whether it is bright or cloudy. On bright days water more; on gray days water less. If possible, use tepid water because icy cold water can shock plants.

Humidity and Air Circulation

A high humidity is not a vital concern when growing geraniums; indeed, too much moisture in the air can curtail rather than help growth. The plants do fine at about 20 percent humidity. On the other hand, avoid a very dry atmosphere, which can kill geraniums.

Good air circulation is of prime concern in the successful culture of geraniums. These plants like a buoyant atmosphere in which air circulates freely. This does *not* mean opening windows and putting plants in drafts in the winter. A small fan going at low speed in the growing area works fine when windows are closed against the cold.

Light and Feeding

Geraniums do best in bright light, even direct light, in the spring and summer. But come winter, give plants all the sun possible or blossoming will be sparse—geraniums must get their share of winter sun. On cloudy days provide artificial light for these plants (they will respond beautifully). More on artificial light in Chapter 9.

When plants are growing well—showing signs of growth—you can add some plant food occasionally. I maintain a feeding schedule of twice a month for my geraniums and use a 5-10-10 plant food. As soon as growth stops in the late fall or early winter, I stop feeding entirely. Every third month I take my plants to the sink and leach them with water. To do this, fill the sink with water and then submerge plants to the pot's rim for about 15 minutes. This helps alleviate any toxic salt buildup from plant foods.

Insects and Disease

Geraniums do have their share of insect problems—aphids and

mealybugs, especially, can attack. Observation is the key to good plant care: catch trouble before it starts. Healthy plants are rarely bothered with insects; it is only the weak ones that are fodder for the bugs.

Bacterial diseases can also be a problem. Such a disease usually manifests itself by stem rot (soft places in the stem). The first symptom is yellowing, and within a day or so water-soaked areas appear. You might try the fungicides zineb and ferbam, but these are not always helpful. It may be best to discard plants with bacterial disease.

Geranium Favorites

Here are some geraniums which will provide much pleasure:

Pelargonium domesticum

Pelargonium domesticum

These plants go by several common names: Lady Washington, Martha Washington, Regal geraniums. By any name they are handsome, with lobed or toothed large leaves and clusters of brilliant flowers on hairy stems. Colors most often seen are red, pink, or purple.

Pelargonium grandiflorui

Pelargonium grandiflorum

    Somewhat large, rangy plants with stout stems and lobed leaves. Flowers in pink shades, moderating to red in some varieties.

Pelargonium hortorum

Pelargonium hortorum

Complex hybrid zonal geraniums with slightly hairy stems and rounded leaves, banded in yellow, cream, white, red, or brown. Lovely flowers in pink, salmon, red, or white. Many varieties available. They usually bloom from early spring through late fall.

Pelargonium peltatum

Pelargonium peltatum

This trailing geranium has shiny, lobed leaves and is commonly called ivy geranium. Handsome 2- to 3-inch clusters of flowers— colors generally red or white, but also pink and lavender.

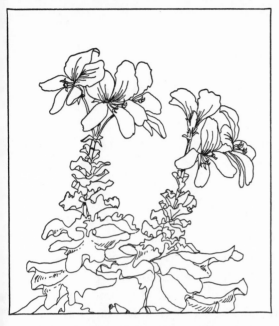

Pelargonium 'Prince Rupert'

Pelargonium 'Prince Rupert'
   A very popular lemon-scented plant also called French Lace,
with somewhat small leaves, variegated green and cream. Rampant
growth. Makes an excellent pot plant. Likes coolness.

Pelargonium vitifolium

Pelargonium vitifolium
   Many varieties; mostly scented. Stems trailing, woody at base.
Flowers small, generally rose-purple or pink.

♫ ♫ Flowering Bulbs

Most of the bulbs described here can be carried over from year to year. They grow almost all year, with just a slight rest period in the winter. Some (in their pots) must be put away in a brown bag for a few months in a cool dark area to regain vigor and get ready for next year's flowers, but others grow on all year.

The secret of growing bulbs is to start them into growth slowly. Start in moderate light in spring or fall—then move to bright light when growth starts. If you have a bulb, rather than a mature plant, give it moderate water, and then increase the amount of the moisture as the leaves start to grow. Feedings once every two weeks with a mild plant food (10–10–5) and a pinch of bonemeal dug into the soil ensure healthy plants. Use a rich soil with good drainage as this is vital for bulbs.

If you have a plant matured from a bulb, grow it until flowering is over; then taper off the watering so the plant can rest for about six weeks. Some plants have to be stored (pot and all) in a paper bag in a cool but not freezing place such as a garage or pantry. Other bulbous plants (and these are mentioned in the plant descriptions below) grow all year.

Most people are somewhat confused about which end of a bulb goes into the planting mix and how deep it should be imbedded. Look at the bulb; most bulbs are tapered. The more pointed tip end is up, and should protrude above the soil line. Generally, but not always, the soil should reach the collar of the plant; it should never be above this area or rot may develop.

Here is a compendium of some bulbous plants and how to grow them. Specific growing hints for each plant are given in detail.

♫ ♫ ♫ ♫

Agapanthus (Lily-of-the-Nile)

These are really outdoor plants but do equally well indoors with
at least four hours of sun. They make a stellar home decoration.
The plants have grassy leaves and the white or blue lilylike flowers
are carried on tall stems. Bulbs are planted in spring or fall in 8- or
12-inch clay pots—they do better if the roots fill the pots. Use a rich
soil that drains readily. Water freely until after flowering and then
let them become somewhat dry through late summer. In winter the
foliage dies down naturally and plants need water only a few times
a month. The dwarf varieties are best for home and can be grown
for several years in the same container. Species is *A. africanus.*

Allium neopolitanum

Allium neopolitanum

This is the flowering onion and it is a fine plant with green strap leaves and lovely umbels of large, starry, white flowers. Pot in a sandy soil and grow at a bright window; give plenty of light. Water sparsely at first but increase moisture as the plant matures. After bloom, keep the soil just barely moist. Can be stored in paper sacks for the winter in a dry dark place or can be kept growing by planting in the garden area.

Amaryllis

Amaryllis (Hippeastrum)

These incredible plants, long-time favorites, have flowers that may be seven inches across—in white, rose, pink, and violet, with red being the most popular color. Bulbs or plants in flower are available at seasonal times from January to March. Plant each bulb in a six- or seven-inch pot, allowing one inch of space between the walls and the bulb. Do not bury the bulb; allow the upper third to stay above the soil line. Moisten the soil, and set the pot in a cool shady place. Grow the plant with just barely moist soil until the flower stalk (which comes before the leaves) is about eight inches tall. Then move the plant into a sunny place and water heavily. Amaryllis take about one month to bear their magnificent flowers.

After the plants bloom, keep the foliage growing so the leaves can manufacture food for next year's flowers. Do not throw the bulb away when the foliage turns brown; keep it in a cool shady place, with the soil almost dry, for about three months, or until you see new growth starting. Then replant the amaryllis in fresh soil (use the same container; amaryllis likes small pots). If you can, put the plant outdoors so it can benefit from fresh rains and warmth; otherwise keep it at a sunny window. In fall, the amaryllis should have cool temperatures (60°F). Increase watering and wait for the next cycle of blooms.

There are many named varieties of amaryllis, but generally they are sold by color rather than by name.

Crocus

Crocus

These favorite flowers, so associated with spring, are featured at florists in season. You can buy the plants already in bloom or plant the corms (similar to bulbs but without scales) and start your own, which is more fun. Flowers can be yellow, white, purple, and even lavender striped. Put six to eight of the small bulbs in a five- or six-inch pot filled with gravel or sandy soil. Water moderately until growth shows. Plants should be in bright light until foliage starts, then move to better light. Flowers last from several days to a few weeks, but after blooming the bulbs must be discarded. *Colchicum autumnale,* also called Crocus, grows from a corm rather than a bulb and blooms in fall. This is so easy to grow that it is sometimes called "magic plant" because it can bloom even out of soil!

Cyclamen

Cyclamen

Plants grow from a corm. They appear in florist shops in February or March. They are low-growing plants with rich green leaves and nodding flowers in white, pink, or red on medium to tall stems. The plants add great glamour to a room; as they are small, they can be used in many areas indoors. Healthy plants bear flowers for a period of several weeks, one following the other in a gay procession of color. When you receive a Cyclamen, put it in a cool place and drench it daily—this plant loves water.

When blooms fade, let the plant die back, and reduce moisture and temperature. If the weather is good, put the pot outside into the ground in a shady place and forget it for a while. In June or July, check to see if new growth has started. If it has, start watering the plant heavily. In September, take the pot from the garden, place it at a sunny window, and continue watering and feeding.

Another way to keep Cyclamens over (and one I did successfully in my Chicago apartment) is to remove the corms from the soil after the bloom time. Put the corms in brown bags and store them in a cabinet in an unheated but not freezing pantry. Let them rest for several months; start them in fresh soil about May. When you restart Cyclamens this way, give them little water for the first few weeks, increasing moisture as growth increases. Always keep Cyclamens out of the direct sun. These are really excellent little plants that can, without too much trouble, be carried over for several years.

Eucharis grandiflora

Eucharis (Amazon lily)

The Amazon lily bears clusters of fragrant star-shaped white flowers on twelve-inch stems, generally in spring or summer. My plant also bloomed once in the winter. Cover bulbs about half their depth with coarse fibrous soil. Water sparingly until growth starts, but always keep the soil somewhat moist. Keep the temperature at 70° to 80°F to encourage the bulbs to sprout. Make sure the plants have good sun all year. During the plant's resting period, decrease waterings and let the temperature drop to 60°F. Do not remove the bulb from the pot; move it to a cool place and keep soil barely moist. In a few months repot in fresh soil, move the pot to warmth, and increase waterings. *E. grandiflora* is the species most offered.

Eucomis punctata

Eucomis (pineapple lily)

This plant thrives indoors in a pot; it has dozens of tiny whitish-green flowers and bright green leaves resembling pineapple foliage, thus the plant's common name. The best species for indoors are *E. undulata* and *E. punctata.*

In the fall, plant bulbs with the crown about one inch deep in a sandy soil. Barely water until February; then increase watering. Keep plants in shade until leaves start growing, at which time plants can be moved into the light. Maintain a night temperature of 50°F. Grow the plant in the same ten-to twelve-inch tub for several years without repotting. Decrease moisture somewhat in the winter, but never let the soil become bone dry.

Freesia

Freesia

Known for their heady fragrance, Freesias are delightful small plants with pretty flowers—they come in many colors—which make nice cut flowers. Put six corms, 1 inch deep and 2 inches apart in a 5- or 6-inch pot, with soil of two parts sandy loam, one part leafmold, and one part old manure or compost. Plant from August to November for January to April bloom. These plants must have coolness to thrive so place them at your coldest window with good light. After the plants bloom, remove bulbs from containers, shake off soil, and keep dry for repotting the next year. Not easy to grow indoors, but not impossible so give them a try.

Haemanthus coccineus

Haemanthus katherinae

Haemanthus (blood lily)

This is a spring or fall flowering amaryllis from South Africa, with 100 or more tiny exquisite red flowers to a globular crown. Bulbs are large so use only one in an eight-inch pot. Plant firmly in a rich, fast-draining soil, leaving the top one-half inch of the bulb protruding. Start bulbs in the fall, with little watering. After growth appears, water copiously, and feed the blood lily every other week with a weak liquid fertilizer. These plants cannot take summer sun, so shade them. In the other seasons sun will not harm Haemanthus.

There are three outstanding types of blood lily. *H. katherinae*, which blooms in spring after the foliage ripens, is a beautiful red. This evergreen plant does not have to be stored away. *H. multiflorus* generally blooms first, and then sprouts foliage. This lily lies dormant in the winter. *H. coccineus* grows all winter but is dormant in summer. *H. multiflorus* and *H. coccineus* need a resting period; barely water them, lower temperatures to 50°F, and make sure plants are in total darkness.

Hyacinth

Hyacinthus

Hyacinths are frequently grown in water alone, or water and pebbles, and bloom with little care. For pot culture use a four- or five-inch container with sandy soil. There are hyacinths for early, midseason, and late color. You can have a succession of fragrant flowers for many months if you stagger the plantings.

Constant moisture and good bright light are necessary for hyacinths. As with most bulbs, start them in coolness (55° to 60°F) and filtered light; as growth progresses, move plants to warmth and more light. Although not overly dramatic, hyacinths are worthwhile for their fragrance and the many colors of the waxy, trumpet-shaped flowers.

Ixia viridiflora

Ixia

Corn lilies are charming cormous plants with slender tall spikes of small, funnel-shaped flowers. Leaves are grassy. Colors of the flowers range from white to pink and red. Use five or six corms to a clay pot and start them from the middle of September to October. Put the container in a very cool (40°F) place to get good root development. If roots are not stocky, growth becomes straggly. Apply water sparsely until leaves are growing; then give routine watering. Flowering takes about six weeks. After plants bloom, bulbs may be stored in the same pot until early fall, in a cool dry place. To start again repot in fresh soil.

Narcissus

Narcissus

Sometimes called paperwhites or (the larger-flowered ones) daffodils, these bulbs bear white or yellow flowers, usually sweetly scented for one season only—then plants are discarded or planted in the garden for color next year. Start six or eight bulbs to a 6-inch container, in pebbles. Keep the gravel moist at all times. Leave them in a shady place until the plants have made foliage growth, then they can be placed at a bright window.

Neomarica caerulea

Neomarica gracilis

Neomarica (Apostle plant)

This is a group of old-fashioned plants with flowers that resemble the iris family, and grassy leaves. Flowers—white-and-violet—appear in winter. Although individual flowers do not last long, the plant blooms for long periods and makes a handsome sight on gray days. Plant rhizomes in sandy soil in 4- or 5-inch containers and give sun and plenty of water. After the plants bloom, rest for about a month with scant waterings and then resume routine moisture. Difficult to find but worth the search. Two best species are *N. caerulea* and *N. gracilis*.

Nerine sarniensis

Nerine

This is sometimes called the Guernsey lily and is a very showy amaryllis with azalealike flowers appearing on leafless stems. Bloom occurs in fall and then leaves start to grow after the flowers fade. There are pink or bright red varieties. Put two or three bulbs in a 6-inch container and grow in the same pot for several years— Nerines like to be rootbound. Use a loose fibrous soil mix that drains readily. Water sparsely at first but, as growth starts, increase moisture and continue to water well through the growing season. Plants need 45°F temperatures and good light to prosper. After bloom, keep the plants growing in good light to naturally ripen the foliage so they can bloom again the next year. When leaves turn yellow and die back, let the soil dry off completely for about six to eight weeks. Then start again.

Ornithogalum arabicum

Ornithogalum

Especially good for cut flowers, Ornithogalums have white or yellow star-shaped flowers on a leafless stalk. The three available species are: *O. arabicum* with white flowers; *O. thyrsoides,* white with a brown spot in center of flower; and *O. aureum,* which has yellow flowers. Plant six or seven bulbs to an 8-inch pot anytime from September to December. Maintain cool temperatures until growth starts, than increase moisture, warmth, and light. Grow in full sun and keep soil evenly moist—they need plenty of water. After plants bloom, allow foliage to ripen naturally. Store them in their pots in a cool dry place (55°F) until fall. Then repot in fresh soil for more flowers.

Oxalis hirta

Oxalis melanosticta

Oxalis

Considered as a weed outdoors, indoors Oxalis yields satiny white, yellow, or red flowers that usually bloom on and off all year. *O. bowieana* has red flowers, *O. cernua* has flamboyant bright yellow flowers, *O. hirta* bears rose-pink flowers, and *O. rubra* has veined rose blooms and *O. melanosneta,* yellow flowers. All are good for cool indoor display. Summer and fall varieties need a winter resting period. In the fall, push three or four corms about two inches below the soil line in an eight-inch pot. Keep soil barely wet until growth starts; then increase watering. Feed plants twice a month with a fertilizer that contains some bonemeal. Ample sunlight will produce an abundance of flowers—flowers don't open on shady days.

Sinningia (gloxinia)

Single or double tubular- or slipper-shaped flowers in vivid colors. There are hybrids that bloom at various times through the year; plants will be in bud or flower when you buy them. The cooler and shadier you keep them, the longer they will last. When you notice flowers fading, reduce watering. Remove the tops after the foliage dies, and store bulbs in a cool shady place for about eight weeks. Keep the soil barely moist. Then repot in fresh soil in a larger pot (one bulb to a pot); set the bulb with the hollow side up, and cover the bulb with soil. Keep the soil evenly moist, at about 60°F. Increase water and warmth when growth starts to flourish, and then get ready for more flowers.

Tulbaghia violacea

Tulbaghia (society garlic)

These wonderful lilies have a 20-inch stem and scented, pale pink to lavender flowers. Arrange several corms to a 6-inch pot. Plant the corms 1-inch apart and half-an-inch deep in sandy soil with a little peatmoss. Give plenty of water and fertilize monthly. Blooms appear on and off from March to November. Very pretty little plants, easy to grow and to multiply. Repot when they become overcrowded.

Vallota speciosa

Vallota (Scarborough lily)

This South African evergreen has clusters of dazzling red flowers in spring or summer, on ten-inch stems. Vallota bulbs are expensive but worth it; try *V. speciosa*. Plants like to be crowded, so use the smallest pot you can. Repot only when absolutely necessary. Plant the bulb with its nose slightly above the soil line. Use a rich, well-draining soil (one-half inch of gravel in the bottom of the pot will ensure good drainage). Keep plants in a bright but not sunny place, water moderately, and feed them every two weeks from spring through fall. Vallotas are slow growing, so do not be surprised if the plant does not bloom the first year.

Veltheimia viridifolia

Veltheimia

This plant from the Cape of Good Hope has pendant yellow flowers tinged red which bloom at the top of tall stalks. *V. viridifolia* is the popular species. Start bulbs in late fall, one to a pot, in loose soil. Plants must have good drainage and fairly dry soil until growth starts. Once growth begins, heavily water the plant through the growing cycle. Feed the plant every two weeks, grow in full sun, and maintain a 55°F temperature. Once the flowers fade, let the leaves turn yellow, then stop watering. Store the bulb in its pot for about two months. Repot in the fall in fresh soil

Zephyranthes candida

Zephyranthes

These are called the rain lily and the zephyr lily. They have grassy foliage and pretty pink or white or orange flowers. In spring pot four or five bulbs to a 6-inch container. Put them in a sunny window and let soil dry out between waterings. In winter, store bulbs in a cool shaded place. Very easy to grow indoors.

∬ ∬ Foliage Plants

Many people only like flowering plants, but still others prefer the foliage favorites that provide a green mantle of color indoors through all the seasons. Finding leafy plants for cool places is not difficult; the problem is that many of our more popular plants, such as Philodendrons, pothos, and Dieffenbachias, just do not perform well in temperatures below 60°F. (Ironically, flowering plants tolerate chill more than the leafy beauties.) But there are foliage plants for indoor splendor that do fine in somewhat cool conditions—most of these have been overlooked through the years, so do not let a new name scare you. These green gems have been in my plant room for many years and have done incredibly well, even in the worst weather.

∬ ∬ ∬ ∬

Some Favorite Foliage Plants

I do not think it is possible to beat Dracaena when it comes to plants that can take hard conditions and still be beautiful home accents. It is primarily *D. marginata* that gets my nod. This lovely decorator plant has long stems that carry thin, dark, and green leaves which are lined red. The plant has a sculptural character and does well in bright light. Let the plant dry out between waterings— this plant needs little attention to thrive. Another good Dracaena indoors is *D. fragrans massangeana*. This is a charming plant with yellow and green leaves that grow in rosettes; the plant can be trained into a tree. Other Dracaenas will grow in cool places as well, but these two are outstanding.

It may come as a surprise, but Citrus plants make very pretty indoor subjects. If necessary, they can adjust to awful conditions and still maintain their bushy greenness. I am especially fond of orange and lemon trees, which do very well in a bright place. Do not expect fruit, however. Water the plants well and then let them dry out between waterings. Occasionally wash leaves with a damp cloth. Citrus can be started from seeds.

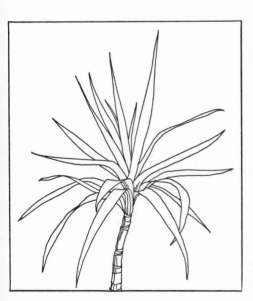

Dracaena fragrans massangeana

Dracaena marginata

Cordyline terminalis

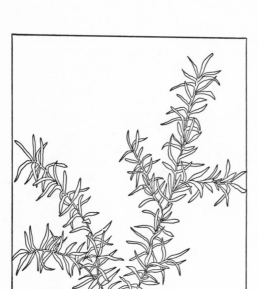

Asparagus sprengeri

To brighten the winter scene I recommend two plants that have been with me for a long time and offer good green color for little effort: the Hawaiian Ti plant, *Cordyline terminalis,* and the splendid *Asparagus sprengeri.* The compact Ti plant is quite popular now, with its lovely dark green leaves lined red, and it never looks straggly or awkward. The asparagus fern, really a lily, is a feathery delight that bears red berries in winter. These plants need bright light and evenly moist soil; both are easy to grow, and low temperatures do not phase them.

Chlorophytum

Coffea arabica

I am also very fond of Chlorophytum, the spider plant, as are thousands of people. This unassuming plant with grassy leaves does well under almost any condition. All it needs is an evenly moist soil and some bright light. Finally, perhaps my other favorite, is the coffee plant, *Coffea arabica*—a delightful, rich-green leaved plant that always seems pretty no matter what the climate outdoors. This one grows readily with an evenly moist soil and good light. Occasionally wash leaves with a damp cloth.

There are of course hundreds of other foliage favorites that can weather the storm; I have not included them in my favorite list merely because of whim. But believe me, they are all very suitable houseplants.

Chamaedorea erumpens

Chamaedorea erumpens

Known as the bamboo palm, this robust plant with tall stems and bamboolike foliage can take 50°F if necessary. Very desirable.

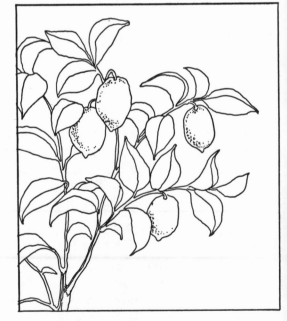

Citrus meyeri

Citrus meyeri

A dwarf Citrus with lovely dark green leaves that does well indoors in cool places. Cut back every spring to encourage new growth.

Fatshedera lizei

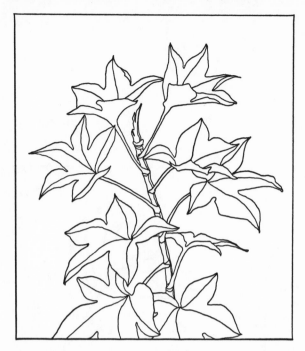

Fatshedera lizei (tree ivy)
   This large plant grows treelike to 36 inches and has large glossy lobed green leaves.

Fatsia japonica

Fatsia japonica (Japanese falsia)
   A large plant with leathery, dark, lobed, shiny green leaves. It is quite decorative in the home. Can grow to 4 or more feet tall.

Howeia forsteriana

Howeia forsteriana (paradise palm)

A beautiful palm with arching fronds and tall stems. Makes a handsome vertical accent. Can tolerate coolness and lives for a long time.

Jasminum humile

Jasminum polyanthum

Jasminum

This overlooked group of plants offers many fine chilly performers, including *J. humile,* which is bushy with yellow flowers, and *J. polyanthum* with fragrant flowers. Jasmine needs some sun and prefers to dry out between waterings.

Pandanus veitchii

Pandanus veitchii (screw pine)

   A splendid performer no matter what the conditions—this plant grows and grows up to 3 to 5 feet high. Pandanus has a rosette shape and long, thin, green leaves edged white. This plant likes a sandy soil; let the soil dry out between waterings.

Rhapsis excelsa

Rhapis excelsa (lady palm)

   This lovely compact palm is not often seen but it is a stellar indoor plant with lovely green leaves of unusual texture. Grows low and bushy, making it very desirable. Tolerates coolness with little problem.

6

Winter

Wonderland

In the dreary winter months, indoor plants are most valued for their flowers, making life brighter during this dull season. There is always something to see and cheer you up when you have winter-blooming beauties. Capturing all this color is not difficult if you follow certain techniques and cultural hints. Here is a host of plants from many plant families—the ones I cultivated through the years, ones that have brought color to my windows on the coldest nights, and can warm your home as well, no matter what the temperature, indoors or out. I have arranged them for color throughout the winter months.

♫ ♫ November Beauties

As gray skies and snowy days come to much of the world, the indoor garden really becomes the focus of attention, where you can spend creative hours tending plants and making sure that there are flowers for the winter. Not too much artificial heat is needed in most regions, but some is. Generally the temperature in my garden room ranges from 55° to 68°F during the day to 50° to 63°F at night in November.

♫ ♫ ♫ ♫

103

Camellia japonica

Camellia japonica

If you have the space and want a showy plant, any variety of the outdoor Camellia shrub will provide weeks of color indoors. Camellia foliage is green, glossy, and leathery. The beautiful flowers are large and waxlike in red, white, or pink. The plants need a rich acid soil with excellent drainage; keep the soil quite moist. Camellias can tolerate temperatures of 40°F if necessary.

Capsicum

The pepper plant is a novelty, with small red fruits that last for weeks. The plant does well with moderate waterings and some sun, but do not try to carry it over from year to year. It is best to buy new plants annually.

Gardenia jasminoides

Gardenia jasminoides

A somewhat large (to thirty inches) evergreen shrub with scented white flowers, Gardenia is difficult to grow because it likes humidity but needs coolness to do well. It also needs a rich acid soil. Do not move plants once they are in bud. Mist leaves and buds frequently and pray—it is worth the trouble.

Eranthemum nervosum

Eranthemum nervosum

Sometimes called blue sage, this provides fine blue color at the windows in November. The tiny flowers almost cover this small (ten-inch) plant. Blue sage needs to be moist all year but needs no rest. It requires all the sun it can get.

Hibiscus

Do try growing Hibiscus because this fine plant can tolerate some coolness and still bloom indoors. The dramatic flowers are large—to five inches across—in orange, red, or yellow. The plants themselves are big, to sixty inches. Although the flowers last only a few days, a healthy plant bears dozens of blooms over a four-week period. Water and fertilize heavily, and prune severely each year.

Ruellia makoyana

Ruellia macrantha

Ruellia makoyana

   The trailing velvet plant is a gem, only ten inches high, with red bell-shaped flowers appearing among the olive-green silver-veined leaves. The foliage is almost as handsome as the flowers. Ruellia needs bright light and does not tolerate dryness, so keep the soil just evenly moist. A somewhat larger plant is *R. macrantha,* with large leaves and rose-colored flowers.

♫ ♫ December Presents

In December you will have to use more artificial heating in the growing area, but do not use too much because the plants that follow can all take coolness and even grow in the snow that is probably a backdrop outside the windows.

Lobularia maritima

Lobularia maritima
The outdoor plant sweet alyssum does very well indoors in chilly places. It is a small trailing plant with heads of fragrant white or lavender flowers. The plants need some sun and moderate watering. Provide good drainage.

Solanum pseudo-capsicum

Solanum pseudo-capsicum

The Jerusalem cherry is a small dark-leaved shrub with white flowers in summer and red berries in winter. It likes bright exposure and does very well in cool conditions. It lasts only a season, but is worth its space.

January is cold and snowy in most of the country, and color at the windows does much to brighten spirits and bring cheer to the home. A flowering plant in the living room or any place is welcome indeed.

Azalea indica

Azalea

Yes, azaleas do grow and bloom indoors, but only the miniatures like *A.* 'Gumpo.' Azaleas need a sandy, acid, and fast-draining soil and water, water, water. Color lasts from January to March. After the flowers fade, dry out the plant somewhat and then put it outside in May. Return the plant to the house in September.

Begonia

I cannot cover this month without mentioning the Christmas begonia, old-fashioned though it may be. This is not an easy plant to grow, but it is not impossible. It is about sixteen inches tall, with lovely pink flowers. After bloom, cut back the plant to six inches or so, and put it outside when the weather becomes warm. Return to the house in September.

Campanula isophylla

Campanula (bellflower)

I have a Campanula that blooms at the end of January, early for most of them but this lovely plant has been with me so long I feel it deserves mention. It has small scalloped leaves and the garlands of blue flowers are dramatic against a gray sky. Grow Campanula—there are dozens of varieties—in your coolest place (about 45°F) and be sure they are in bright light.

Rhododendron

Rhododendron

Rhododendrons are popular outdoor plants but indoors they can be beautiful too—if you can provide them with acid soil and very cool temperatures of say, 45°F. So these fine examples of nature are very much for unheated rooms. There are dozens of varieties—some bloom early, some later in the year, but all are beautiful. The white or red varieties are especially pleasing to my eye, but pink or variegated colors may appeal to you.

♫ ♫ February Follies

In February nature is at a standstill outdoors, but inside many houseplants are in full color and others are starting to bear new growth—little shoots and sprouts here and there.

Arthropodium cirrhatum

Arthropodium cirrhatum
  A member of the lily family, this has tall spikes of white flowers on twenty-four inch plants. It needs considerable moisture while it is growing, but after the bloom keep the plants somewhat dry. It is easy to grow in cool spots.

Cyclamen

Do not forget Cyclamen for those cool windows. These fourteen-inch plants with handsome foliage bear lovely pink or white flowers on tall stems. Drench the plants daily because they are thirsty beggars. If you want to hold them over, store the pots in paper bags in a dark cool place, after the plants flower. Take out the plants and repot them in fresh soil in eight or nine weeks.

Daphne odorata

Daphne odorata

The fragrant Daphne is a tough plant to grow inside but worth the time and effort because this twenty-inch-tall shrub has handsome foliage and lovely pink flowers in the winter. Grow it in a sandy soil that has perfect drainage. This plant likes it cool, cool, cool.

Jatropha pandurifolia

Jatropha pandurifolia

This is another fine indoor plant for cool places. It is grown more for its lovely scarlet flowers than its foliage.

Lantana montevidensis

Lantana montevidensis

Lantana is a winter favorite of mine. This trailing plant (to thirty inches) has fuzzy green leaves and clusters of fine lilac flowers. It needs plenty of water and some sun and is a perfect plant for cool places.

Pelargonium 'Alphonse Richard'

   This geranium is a tall grower that produces fine red flowers. Soak the soil and then let it dry out between waterings. It needs some sun.

Petrea volubilis

Petrea volubilis (purple wreath, queen's wreath)

   The lavender and violet-purple blossoms look a bit like Verbena. Thick oblong leaves grow on the woody stems of this climber.

Reinwardtia indica

Reinwardtia indica

Yellow flax is seldom seen, yet this is another star cool-house performer. It grows to twenty inches, with dark green leaves and large yellow flowers that look like Petunias. Blooms appear at the tips of shoots on and off through the dull months. In time plants become straggly, so pinch shoots occasionally to induce a nice shapely growth.

Rosa 'Tom Thumb'

Rosa 'Tinker Bell'

Rosa

Ideally, some fall and winter blooming miniature roses should be in the indoor garden. These tiny replicas of the larger garden types do bloom indoors with temperatures of about 50° to 55°F. They do have their problems though—red spiders love them and are difficult to eliminate; try the old-fashioned remedies mentioned in Chapter 5.

Stephanotis floribunda

Stephanotis floribunda

Another fine cool plant, its fragrant white flowers perfume the home in late summer. Grow in an unheated 50°F place. Can grow as a vine or shrub.

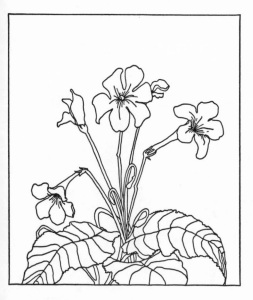

Streptocarpus

Streptocarpus

Not to be overlooked are the Cape primroses from the Gesneriad family. These fine plants can, if absolutely necessary, grow in 58°F. Their flowers, appearing on and off through the year (but mainly winter), are colorful and always desirable. Don't get water on the leaves or rot may occur.

7
Keeping Plants Healthy

An outdoor garden may be plagued with pests, but the indoor garden is usually free of insects. Tons of insecticides are sold, but for emergency use you need only buy a bottle of Malathion. Old-fashioned preventatives are the mainstay of my battle with bugs. If the culture is good and the plants prosper, if you carefully wash foliage frequently (or at the very least wipe it with a damp rag), and if you inspect all new arrivals, your insect problem is virtually eliminated. However, occasionally a fungus disease strikes a plant. In this case, discard the plant rather than risk having other plants in your collection contract the disease. (This often costs less money than buying the proper fungicide.) Often what looks like an insect attack on a plant may be merely the result of poor culture. In this case, spraying with insecticides is futile and can be harmful to the plant. Before you buy insecticides, decide just what you are fighting—aphids, mealybugs bugs, fungus—and then find the appropriate remedy.

If your plants are attacked by insects, try hosing them down with clear water every other day for a few weeks, or use Black Leaf 40 solution. If insects still persist, then apply Malathion.

ℐ ℐ ℐ ℐ

𝒮 𝒮 Signs of Culture Trouble

Spindly growth or wilts: temperature or light is not to the plant's liking.

Foliage withers: probably caused by a cold draft being directly on a plant, a drastic change in temperature, or watering with very cold water.

Leaves with dry areas: usually caused by impurities in the air, such as gasoline or industrial fumes.

Leaves with burnt or scorched areas: direct sunlight magnified by a defect in window glass can act like a magnifying glass and burn up leaves.

Buds that fail to open: usually caused by too much sun or too dry an atmosphere. Mist buds with water to soften casings. If buds drop, increase humidity.

𝒮 𝒮 𝒮 𝒮

SYMPTOM	PROBABLE CAUSE	REMEDY
No new growth	Too much water; soil is compacted; roots are decayed	Repot in fresh soil mixture; adjust watering practices
Stems or leaves turn yellow	Iron deficiency from soil being too alkaline	Test the pH of soil; add iron chelates if reaction is neutral to alkaline
Pale color on new growth	Root injury	Trim away dead or damaged roots; repot plant
Elongated growth	Not enough light	Move plant to location with more light
Failure to bloom, or very few flowers	Too much nitrogen; no winter rest; or both	Use fertilizer low in nitrogen and higher in phosphorus; give the plant a winter rest
Flower buds drop	Temperature is low or too fluctuating; plant is in draft	Move plant to warmer, draft-free location
Soft or mushy growth	Too much moisture; temperature too low	Reduce moisture, cut away soft parts, and dust cuts with Captan
Plant has glassy, translucent look beginning in fall or winter	Frost damage	No cure; to prevent, keep plant dry, and be sure it is not subjected to too low temperatures

♫ ♫ What Insects to Look For

Mealybugs, aphids, and red spider mites are the insects that do the most damage to houseplants. Mealybugs and aphids can be seen, but the microscopic red spider mites are barely visible to the naked eye and thus do the most damage because they get a good foothold before they are detected. White flies, thrips, scale, and slugs are other pests that occasionally attack houseplants.

Mealybugs are oval insects covered with what looks like white cotton. They gather on stems, leaves, and the undersides of leaves. They harbor their young in leaf axils. The insects suck the plant sap, which results in undersize foliage and flowers. Eliminate mealybugs with a solution of Black Leaf 40 or Malathion.

Aphids are pear-shaped and soft-bodied plant lice that crawl all over a plant. They multiply rapidly and cause leaves to become spindly and deformed.

Red spider mites gather on the undersides of leaves and weave a fine web; the leaves become brown and finally drop off.

Spider mites thrive on hot still air. To control them, spray foliage with water or use Dimite, a miticide.

White flies are tiny white insects that lay quantities of eggs on leaf undersides. The foliage then turns yellow and drops off. Spray with Malathion.

Scale are hard-shelled, readily-seen insects that attach themselves to leaves or stems. They suck the juice from the plant, causing the foliage to turn pale. To get rid of scale, rub them off, pick them off with a toothpick, or use Malathion.

Thrips are tiny yellow, black, or brown insects that move quickly. A heavy infestation leaves foliage streaked and silvery. Spray with Malathion.

Slugs hide under stones, leaves, and pots. They rarely venture forth during the day; they feed at night and eat ragged holes in leaves. Bug Getta is an effective control.

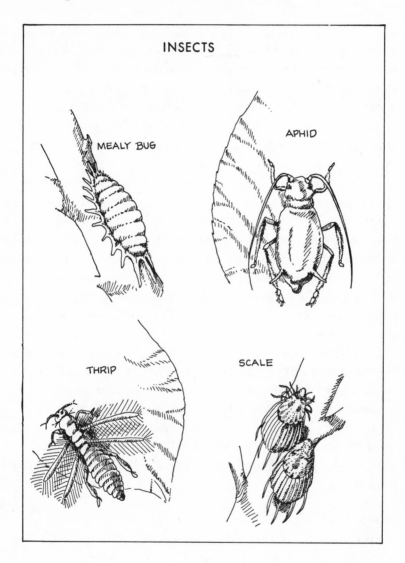

INSECTS

MEALY BUG

APHID

THRIP

SCALE

✍ ✍ Plant Diseases

If plants are well cared for they rarely develop diseases. Still, just in case, it is wise to know what to do; no one wants a costly plant ruined by fungus or botrytis, and a little knowledge can help you save infected plants. Most diseases that do occur will be minor, but if left unchecked they can become major concerns.

Ailments that strike plants are manifested in visible symptoms—spots, rot, mildew, and so on. Many plant diseases may result in similar external symptoms, so it is important to identify the specific disease to ensure positive remedies.

Unfavorable growing conditions—too little or too much humidity, or too much feeding—can help to contribute to disease, but mainly diseases are caused by bacteria and fungi. Bacteria enter the plant through naturally minute wounds and small openings. Inside, they multiply and start to break down plant tissue. Animals, soil, insects, water, and dust carry bacteria that can attack plants. If you have touched a diseased plant, you, too, can carry the disease to healthy ones. Soft roots, leaf spots, wilts, and rots are some diseases caused by bacteria.

Fungi, like bacteria, enter a plant through a wound or a natural opening or by forcing their entrance directly through plant stems or leaves. Spores are carried by wind, water, insects, people, and equipment. Fungi multiply rapidly in shady, damp conditions rather than in hot, dry situations; moisture is essential in their reproduction. Another reason for having good air circulation around your plants. Fungi cause rusts, mildew, some leaf spot, and blights.

Fungicides

Fungicides are chemicals that kill or inhibit the growth of bacteria and fungi. They come in ready to use dust form, in wettable powder, or soluble forms to mix with water and use as a spray. The following is a brief resume of the many fungicides available:

Captan: An organic fungicide that is generally safe and effective for the control of many diseases.

Ferbam: A very effective fungicide against rusts.

Karanthane: Highly effective for many types of powdery mildew.

Sulfur: This is an old and inexpensive fungicide and still good; it controls many diseases.

Zineb: Used for many bacterial and fungus diseases.

Benomyl: A systemic used for many bacterial and fungus maladies.

As with all chemicals, use as directed on the package and with extreme caution. Keep all containers out of reach of children and pets.

♫ ♫ Old-Fashioned Remedies

I have done indoor gardening for twenty years, long before modern insecticides hit the market, so I prefer to use old-fashioned methods of eliminating insects from plants. They are perhaps not as thorough as chemicals, but they are safe and avoid noxious odors in the house.

Handpicking: Hardly pleasant, but it can be done with a toothpick.

Soap and water: For many insects, such as aphids and mealybugs, a solution of ½ pound of laundry soap (not detergent) to 1 gallon water works fine. Spray or douse the mixture on bugs and repeat the applications every three to six days for three weeks.

Alcohol: Alcohol on cotton swabs will effectively remove mealybugs and aphids. Apply it directly to the insect.

Tobacco: Use a solution of old tobacco from cigarettes steeped in water for several days. Gets rid of scale. Repeat several times.

Water spray: This may sound ineffective, but it works if used frequently and with strong enough force to wash away insects.

Wipe leaves frequently: This simple step really goes a long way to reduce insect problems. It washes away eggs before they hatch.

8
Propagation

There are many ways to increase your plants from those you already have, including cuttings, seeds, and air layering.

♫ ♫ Cuttings

Stem and leaf cuttings almost always give you new plants. I use pure sand as a rooting medium, although perlite and other mediums that encourage root development can be tried too. An aquarium or a fruit box is a good propagating case. Warmth is necessary for starting plants, 68°F at night, 78°F during the day, with 60 to 80 percent humidity inside the case. Use a glass cover to enclose the cuttings, but lift the cover occasionally to permit circulation of air because a very damp atmosphere is harmful. Keep the cuttings moist but never soggy. It takes a few weeks for some cuttings to root, months for others.

For stem cuttings, snip the stems from the tip growth. Select cuttings from sturdy stems or branches or from the base of the plant. Make an opening about 1 inch deep in the sand, insert the cutting into the sand, and pack the medium around it.

With leaf cuttings—for example, rex Begonias, African violets— cut across the leaf veins in several places on the underside. I use a sharp razor blade. Put the leaves right side up, flat on the sand, in the cutting box, with the stems in the sand. Be sure the leaf is in contact with the sand. Plantlets soon appear along the cuts and draw nourishment from the old leaf. When the new plants can be handled easily, cut them from the parent leaf and pot them separately. Leaf cuttings taken in spring and summer are more apt to produce plants than those taken in autumn or winter.

🍃 🍃 Seeds

With some plants you must sow seeds to get new . plants. Although this is not an exacting procedure, it is not always successful. It is the only way to have some hard-to-find plants or the stock of a favorite plant to give to friends.

Sow seeds in the late winter to early spring. Use shallow bulb pans or Azalea pots rather than flats. When planting seeds, provide drainage as you would for any potted plants. Fill the container with equal parts of loam, sand, and peat moss. Tap the bottom of the pot on the table surface to settle the soil and eliminate air spaces. Try to get the surface as level as possible. Soak the soil, and then scatter seeds on top of the soil or imbed them slightly below the soil line, depending on the type of plant being grown. (Very fine seeds need no covering; merely set them on top of soil.)

Provide seeds with a warm temperature, a humid atmosphere, and a shady location. Put the pans or pots in an aquarium or any glass container on a moist gravel bed. Cover the top of the container with aluminum foil or a dark cloth. When the seeds start to sprout, remove them from the container and put them in a bright but not sunny place. Mist the soil frequently, but do not overwater. In a few days set the seedlings in sun or shade, depending on the requirements of the plants. When the first leaves appear, replant the seedlings in individual pots with the appropriate soil. Water sparingly at first, but do not let the soil dry out. Keep the plants in good light and out of drafts.

ℐ ℐ Air Layering

Woody stemmed plants like Dieffenbachia and Philodendron are best propagated by air layering. Peel off the soft tissue of the plant below a leaf joint (swelling on the stem). Then scrape away a ring of outer tissue, and wrap a clump of spaghnum moss around the bare wood. Keep the moss moist. Cover the ring and moss with polyethylene plastic tied at both ends. When the moss is filled with roots, cut off the new plant below the root ball and plant it. For the first planting, put the fledgling in a very porous mixture. After a few months, transplant it to a regular pot and soil.

ℐ ℐ Division

Plants that grow in clumps—some orchids, ferns—need only to be separated for new ones. Merely pull apart each clump with its individual root system, or with some plants, use a sharp knife to separate the clumps. Pot the new plants, and give them a thorough soaking. Place the plants in bright light until they are established, and then provide as much humidity as possible.

ℐ ℐ ℐ ℐ

PROPAGATION

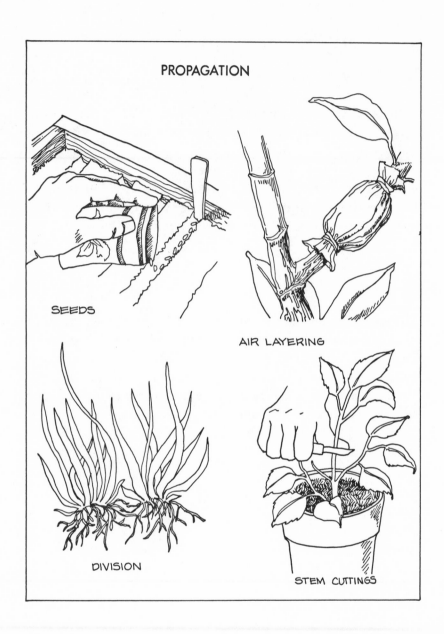

SEEDS

AIR LAYERING

DIVISION

STEM CUTTINGS

9
Artificial
Light

If window space is limited in your home, or if other buildings shut out light, you can still have houseplants—artificial light makes it possible. Indoor gardens under artificial light can be in closets, basements, attics, under stairs, or in the pantry. You can make your own arrangements with used light fixtures and home-made trays, or you can buy one of the commercial table models or movable carts.

The visible colors of light are violet, blue, green, yellow, orange, and red; there are some invisible rays also. Plants use various parts of the color spectrum at various times in their life cycle. Generally, plants absorb more red and blue light than green and yellow. Scientists have discovered that the red and blue light stimulate plant growth. Blue light promotes the production of sugar and starches (photosynthesis), and red light causes germination and also promotes the production of plant growth. Red light also controls a plant's photoperiodism (the response of organisms to the relative length of day and night). Plants exposed to their proper photoperiod grow faster and bloom better. Some plants need long duration (fourteen to eighteen hours); some intermediate (twelve to eighteen hours); and others require short photoperiods (ten to thirteen hours). Therefore, the amount of time plants should be exposed to artificial lamps varies according to the plant.

Whether you make your own unit or buy one, remember that

artificial-light gardens need humidity, ventilation, and some con-trol of day and night temperature. The garden should be in a place where there is easy access to water and where you can tend plants without bumping into furniture.

If the garden is in the living room, dining room, or kitchen, where appearance is important, it must be used decoratively. Base-ments and attics are more suitable areas for experimentation and they usually have more space. The basement is the most popular place for an artificial-light garden because it provides many of the environmental conditions needed by plants—stable air, moderate temperatures—and usually there is no harm from water splashing or dripping on the floor.

⟋⟋ ⟋⟋ What to Grow

Almost any plant can be grown under artificial light; however, some fare better than others. African violets, gloxinias, Philoden-drons, some Begonias, and seedling orchids have done remarkably well for me. Bromeliads, cacti, and succulents did not show any marked improvements under lights from their counterparts grown in windowsills. Choose plants that appeal to you and try them; experimenting is half the fun of this kind of gardening.

Humidity, temperature, ventilation, and moisture factors must be carefully controlled, perhaps with more care than if you are growing plants at windows, because plants grow all the time in artificial gardens. At windows, if there is a series of cloudy days and you forget to water plants, little harm is done. Ventilation is vital for plants in fluorescent gardens. In an area where there are many plants together, a small fan or open windows (weather permitting) is necessary.

⟋⟋ ⟋⟋ ⟋⟋ ⟋⟋

♫ ♫ Kinds of Lamps

There is a bewildering array of fluorescent lamps. Some are cool white; others are daylight, warm white, or natural light. Tubes designed specifically for plant growth, that is, with more red and blue light, are most popular with growers. These are Plant-Gro by Westinghouse Electric and Gro-Lux by Sylvania Electric. Duro-Lite Lamps Natur-escent tubes for plant growth are full-color energy tubes and use other elements of light beyond the basic red and blue colors; they produce true color rendition and do not give off the purple light typical of the other lamps.

It is difficult to suggest which lamps to use. I have been successful growing plants with a combination of two forty-watt cool white tubes and two forty-watt Gro-Lux tubes.

ACCENT LIGHTING

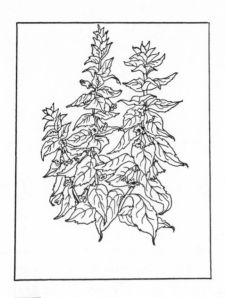

10

Some Like

It Hot

It may seem superfluous to include a chapter on warmth-loving plants in a book on plants for cool houses. But it really is not because if you know the warm plants you can avoid buying them and thus save yourself money and time. And if you do happen to have some tropical beauties struggling at your chilly windows, you will want to keep these plants thriving. It is not easy, but you *can* save these plants through the chilly winters.

♪ ♪ The Sun Worshippers

Tropical plants like gingers, bananas, and some Begonias do require warmth (78°F by day and a few degrees cooler at night). Without it they simply do not grow. Gesneriads are another group of plants that revel in warmth and this includes a great many plants from the following groups:

Achimenes (magic flower, nut orchid, widow's tear)
Aesychnanthus (lipstick plant, basketvine)
Columnea
Episcia (flame violet)
Kohleria
Rechsteineria (cardinal flower, Brazilian edelweiss, double-decker plant)

Saintpaulia (African violet)
Smithiantha (temple bells)
Streptocarpus (Cape primrose)

These tropical beauties in their native habitat abound on forest floors in humid heat and so have a difficult time adjusting to cool evenings. I have found that few of my Gesneriads make it through winter so I strongly urge you to avoid these plants if your home is cool. The one exception is African violets—newer varieties seem to have more stamina to get through a tough winter.

Anthuriums and Alocasias are plants with very handsome foliage and recently these have been offered in great numbers to the public. Unfortunately, they, too, are jungle denizens and like it hot and humid. It is best to forget about growing these in cooler homes, beautiful though they may be. A few evenings at 60°F and the plants will be injured. Another group of plants that have become popular in recent years is the Marantas (prayer plants). These have exquisite foliage but again must have very warm conditions to survive.

Sun-lovers such as Dipladenia, Bougainvillea, Thunbergia (black-eyed Susan vine) and Costus to mention only a few are other plants to be avoided in cool conditions. This is surely a shame because these are very beautiful flowering gems that many people are fond of. Yet, why bring plants into your home to kill them? It makes better sense to avoid these tropicals.

Begonias constitute a large group of very fine indoor plants but most are warm-growing plants. Although there are some exceptions (and these plants were mentioned in a previous chapter) it would be wise to steer clear of most Begonias if your growing conditions are cool (less than 60°F at night).

I have mentioned many orchids that can grow in chilly places but there are also many orchids that cannot take cold. Cattleyas and Laelias for example really like it warm; so do most Epidendrums and Indian-type Dendrobiums. Stanhopeas are other orchids that prefer the heat. Avoid all these groups if possible.

♫ ♫ Protection

With less heat and light, heat-loving plants do not grow as readily as they do with optimum conditions. This means that the plants cannot make food as readily as they do under normal conditions. If you flood plants with water or feed them to try and make them grow, you can kill them. So follow two basic rules during cooler times: (1) water plants sparsely, and (2) do not feed them.

Another vital part of keeping your warm plants with you in cold situations is making sure the humidity (the moistness in air) does not get too high. High humidity coupled with gray days and coolness can cause fungus diseases, so keep humidity at 20 to 30 percent.

In cool conditions it helps to keep a flow of air circulating through the growing area. I solved this problem by running a small fan set at low speed most of the day. A good current of air helps plants, but avoid drafts. On very cold nights move your sun worshippers away from the windows. Even if you have caulked the windows to conserve heat, there is more cold near the panes than away from them. Moving plants just a few inches away from the glass helps considerably. If cold is severe (and it can be in such places as Chicago, with nights often 10° or 15°F below zero outside), put newspaper over the windows to help keep heat in. This is time consuming but worth it for a few nights if weather conditions warrant it.

If, in spite of all your precautions, the growing area drops to below 50°F, consider leaving on a few lamps. An ordinary forty-watt incandescent bulb left on at about thirty inches from the plants provides considerable heat; two or three of these lamps burning does not cost that much money. Another trick to use in cold situations is to move the warmth-loving houseplants to higher positions, because warm air rises. Thus, at ceiling height the temperature is somewhat warmer than at table height. In my kitchen I have several plants hanging in baskets near the ceiling.

These are plants like Clerodendrum, and Mandevilla, which simply cannot tolerate temperatures below 60°F at night.

If your plants are in plastic pots, it might be wise to repot some of them in clay ones. Plastic holds water longer than clay, so the soil can get soggy and cause problems. Rooms like the kitchen and bathroom are always somewhat warmer than other rooms during very cold nights because these rooms are used more. I urge you to move some of your more tropical plants into the kitchen, where they will survive, look good, and provide pleasant decoration. And bathroom gardens are now becoming very popular—there is good humidity in this room and plants help soften the severe lines of bathroom fixtures.

If all this moving about of plants seems like work, it is, but it is worth it because once spring comes you need not do it. The protection only applies in the cold months, when heat is at a premium.

♫ ♫ In Summary

The sun-worshipping plants provide lovely accents in the home or greenhouse so you do not want to lose them. I have mentioned several ways to protect warm plants you have. Just remember that though none of the methods are foolproof they should help you to keep the plants you have. For the future—as long as the cost of energy keeps soaring—it seems the most prudent way of good indoor gardening is to select those cool-liking plants we have discussed in previous chapters. Then you need not worry about losing beautiful plants when it gets cold outside or inside.

♫ ♫ ♫ ♫

11
Greenhouse
Growing

People with greenhouses, who usually had what were called "stove" plants in the old days, have been hard hit by the energy shortage and high cost of warming their plant palaces. Many of my friends have discarded (with sorrow) their beautiful plants and others have instituted some ingenious methods of converting the greenhouse into a less energy-expensive structure. There are several ways of having a greenhouse with beautiful plants and of still conserving energy.

Greenhouses are all glass and glass is a poor insulator. Thus gardens under glass can and do require excessive amounts of heating in cold climates. However let's look at some ways to keep the heat *in* the greenhouse—this encompasses what is commonly known today as passive solar energy. And also let us look at a real heat-saving type of greenhouse called the pit greenhouse.

♫ ♫ Ways to Conserve Heat

If you already have an existing greenhouse that is single glazed (one thickness of glass, the way most were built), you can tape plastic sheeting to the glass, leaving an air space of one-inch between the glass and the plastic. This creates an insulating space that can help save heat. It is a chore to apply the plastic and it really has to be replaced yearly but it does help save heat escaping from the glass area.

Applying one of the principles of solar heating, you might paint the north inside wall of your greenhouse a dark color to absorb the heat from the sun during the day. At night this heat will naturally help warm the glassed-in garden.

Another way to keep out old man winter is to apply heavy material to windows in a drapery fashion—this too acts as insulation but of course it is tedious to have to open and shut the drapery each day. More practical than this method, it seems, would be to leave a few lamps on in the greenhouse—two or three 60-watt light bulbs. It would cost less for this energy than to keep stoking the furnace. The heat from the incandescent bulbs would keep the chill away. Obviously, if you are just building a greenhouse it makes good sense to select one that is double-glazed. Two pieces of glass with an air space acts as insulation and can save as much as 30 percent in heating costs.

On very cold nights, newspapers or cardboards set against the windows and taped into place help to keep the chill out to some extent. It also keeps out light but this is generally all right for a few nights.

If you really want to save energy costs, the perfect greenhouse is the one called an underground pit—here the major part of the greenhouse is built under the ground with only the eaves on top. I had one of these. The growing area was five feet below grade level and this old-fashioned type greenhouse needed no heat at all on the coldest nights here (about 30°F). In northern climates, friends with underground greenhouses told me they used very little heat even when temperatures dropped below the zero mark.

In the underground greenhouse the earth acts as a blanket and insulator and it is amazing what you can grow without any artificial heat; this is a very old way of growing plants and a good one for today's energy problems. The frame of the greenhouse is all glass in a standard A-shaped configuration. Most of these energy-saving glass gardens are somewhat small; mine was 8 feet across and 15 feet long.

ℐ ℐ Growing In Cool Conditions

Growing plants in the cool greenhouse is different from plant cultivation in a temperate or warm house. With less heat and light, plants grow slowly and thus the usual routine of copious watering and feeding should be adjusted. In short, water less and feed very little.

Be careful about getting humidity too high in the cool greenhouse as this (coupled with gray days) can cause fungus disease in plants. It is best to keep humidity at about 20 to 30 percent on very cold nights.

While we are trying to conserve heat, it may seem foolish to suggest that you keep some fresh air moving in the glass garden but a good buoyant atmosphere is necessary for healthy plant growth. Keep ventilators open a crack during the day so air can circulate— very few plants grow in stagnant conditions. Good air circulation will also help to prevent insects from accumulating in the garden. It is in closed atmospheres that pests proliferate.

Any of the plants mentioned in Chapter 5 will do well indeed in a greenhouse and can be grown under glass. In addition you can also start seed in greenhouses and do other propagation techniques as explained in Chapter 8.

ℐ ℐ ℐ ℐ

12
More
Cool Plants
To Grow

I have covered my favorite plants in the main sections of this book. Now we come to other plants I have grown through the years that will adjust, if necessary, to cool temperatures. While these may not be my favorites, they may be yours and certainly should be grown. So here are other cool-growing indoor lovelies you might want to try. These plants are available from your usual suppliers and should also succeed beautifully in less than optimum conditions—that is, with less heat than usual.

The plants are arranged in two groups—those for very cool places (unheated rooms) and others for intermediate places where there is some artificial heat. Where possible I have included some cultural notes but generally what follows is a description of the plants themselves.

✍ ✍ Plants For Very Cool Places

You can try these in unheated areas; most can tolerate temperatures as low as 45°F at night.

✍ ✍ ✍ ✍

Acacia armata

This is really a shrub or tree and has small leaves which are not overly attractive. The vibrant yellow flowers are very desirable and occasionally do bloom indoors near bright light. Likes a thorough drying out between waterings.

Acanthus mollis

Known for its very large and handsome foliage, this erect plant (to about 48 inches) makes a handsome decorator subject. Fine spires of whitish-purple flowers in summer.

Brunfelsia floribunda

A very pretty but somewhat temperamental plant that I have never been successful with, but it might grow for you. The plant has lovely foliage and fine purple flowers.

Chrysanthemum

Chrysanthemums

Outdoor plants, these have finally moved into the home. Numerous varieties offered by florists at seasonal times. As indoor plants they can add color to cool apartments and houses for several weeks. Worth the space but don't count on them as permanent residents.

Clivia miniata

This outstanding pot plant, also called kafir lily, which I grew years ago, is a favorite in England and deserves more recognition here. Its long strap leaves are handsome and the orange flowers in large clusters exquisite. One not to be missed. Does beautifully in coolness.

Convallaria majalis

The beautiful sweet pea of the florist trade. Grows from a corm and has broad green leaves and tiny scented white flowers. An excellent cut flower.

Exacum affine

Exacum affine
A small plant, to 14 inches, this Arabian violet has dark green leaves and fine blue flowers. It has never been a favorite of mine (my plants always died) but might be a good one for you.

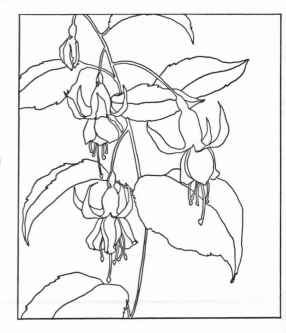

Fuchsia

Fuchsia
These popular plants have bushy or trailing growth and pendent flowers. Many varieties in many color combinations. Likes and prospers in coolness.

Hydrangea

Hydrangea

A popular florist plant available at seasonal times. Grows well in coolness. Flowers in compact clusters. Very pretty.

Ixia

A group of small bulbous plants with grassy foliage and small flowers. Good for the adventurer.

Ixora coccinea

Ixora coccinea

A handsome compact plant with dark green leaves and clusters of small red flowers. Can succeed in coolness, if necessary. Provides handsome color.

Lapeirousia cruenta
A very handsome, small, 10-inch plant with fine red flowers. Plant five or six tiny bulbs to a 6-inch pot of rich soil. Very pretty and loves it cold.

Masdevallia coccinea
A fine small orchid to 10 inches with leathery, spatula-shaped leaves and brilliant red flowers shaped like tiny kites.

Masdevallia touarensis
Similar to the above in size and shape, these plants have white flowers; thrive in coolness, and will bloom in less-than-good light.

Oncidium splendidum
A very amenable 30-inch orchid with hard, leathery, solitary leaves and yellow and brown flowers in abundance. Needs rest after blooming. Carry dry for about a month.

Pleione
Many species of this orchid group make fine cool houseplants. Flowers are large and breathtaking—mostly purple. Grows from a small cormlike tuber. Dies down part of year. Nice for something unusual.

Rivina humilis
A pretty plant with handsome oval leaves and drooping clusters of white flowers followed by red berries. Called the rouge plant.

Rochea coccinea
A shrubby 20-inch succulent with showy red flowers. Use well-drained sandy soil and give full sun.

Vanda parishi
This is a small Vanda—to 16 inches—and a mighty fine orchid. Has straplike leaves and multicolored small flowers. Very amena-

ble to coolness and grows well indoors. Sure to bloom in good light.

♫ ♫ Plants For Partially Heated Rooms

Temperatures must not go below 50°F at night.

Abutilon hybridum
This is a rangy plant growing tall, to 48 inches, with scalloped leaves and very handsome bell-shaped orange flowers. Very pretty; likes lots of moisture. Called flowering maple.

Acalypha hispida
The chenille plant is small, to 14 inches, and has showy strings of red flowers that are borne from leaf axils.

Agave marginata
The old-fashioned century plant; a 30-inch rosette of green leaves. One of the easiest plants to grow.

Ananas comosus variegatus
A 30-inch Bromeliad called pineapple, with beautiful yellow-green-pink foliage. A very handsome plant that will take some coolness.

Ascocentrum ampullaceum
A lovely orchid with straplike leaves and small clusters of per-fectly beautiful cerise flowers. Very desirable. Easy to grow.

Beloperone guttata
The popular shrimp plant prefers warmth but if mature will adjust to cool conditions. Plants have papery leaves and colorful bracts. Cut back tip ends occasionally to encourage growth.

Bifrenaria harrisoniae

Another orchid and a fine one for cool places. Leaves are large and handsome; flowers dramatic—rose-pink with darker markings. Very desirable.

Calanthe

This is an unusual group of mostly deciduous orchids that bear handsome white-and-red flowers on leafless stalks. Plants adjust readily to coolness.

Crossandra infundibuliformis

With shiny green leaves and lovely orange flowers, these plants from India prefer warmth but will after a time adjust to cooler temperatures and still grow well.

Hypocyrta strigillosa

The popular goldfish plant, this sprawling 24-inch plant has small, leathery, dark green leaves and orange flowers. Unusual and generally easy to grow.

Impatiens

Impatiens

These shade-loving plants from the garden do equally well indoors in cool places. Plants have handsome dark green foliage and lovely red or pink flowers. Many new varieties available. Good pot plants.

Kaempferia roscoeana

An unusual tuberous plant; grows only 14 inches high, with lovely broad-leaved foliage and fine lavender flowers—a few a day all summer. Let the tuber die down in winter and store in paper sack in cold place (45°F).

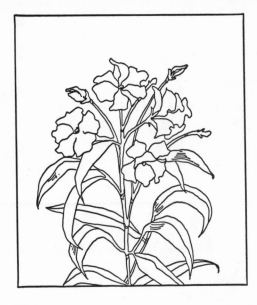

Nerium oleander album

Nerium

Best known as oleander, these bushy plants have lovely small flowers and make handsome house plants. Grow moist and in bright light. Will tolerate low temperatures easily.

Plumbago

Plumbago capensis

With tiny blue flowers, Plumbago does well in coolness and blooms on and off throughout the year. Cut back tip ends somewhat in early spring to encourage growth.

Primula

Primula

These primroses are very pretty little plants for cool places. Give sun and plenty of water. Pick off faded flowers to keep new flowers coming.

Saintpaulia

These are the popular African violets and many of the newer varieties do very well in low temperatures. Many types available and all very pretty. Good windowsill plants.

Schizocentron elegans

Don't let the long name deter you from getting this plant. Called Spanish shawl, it is very handsome with tiny dark green leaves and lovely cerise flowers. Will tolerate coolness if necessary.

Sedum sieboldi

A 16-inch succulent with handsome leathery green leaves and fine pink flowers; very easy to grow.

Spathiphyllum

Hardly seen but certainly worth space in the indoor garden is Spathiphyllum with lovely dark green leaves and Jack-in-the-pulpit type white flowers; very hardy plant.

Appendices

♫ ♫ Plant Suppliers

The mail-order suppliers below carry all types of plants. Almost every one will furnish a catalogue, but many do make a nominal charge for it. The fee is usually refundable, though, on the first purchase of plants.

Alberts & Merkel Bros. Inc.
2210 S. Federal Highway
Boynton Beach, FL 33435

Arthur Eames Allgrove
Box 459
Wilmington, MA 01887

Barrington Greenhouses
860 Clemente Rd.
Barrington, NJ 08016

Buell's Greenhouses
Eastford, CT 06242

Cactus by Mueller
10411 Rosedale Highway
Bakersfield, CA 93307

Cooks Geranium Nursery
712 N. Grand
Lyons, KS 67554

Fischer's Greenhouses
Dept. HC
Linwood, NJ 08221

Henrietta's Cactus Nursery
1345 N. Brawley
Fresno, CA 93705

Great Lakes Orchids
P.O.B. 1114
Monroe, MI 48161

Logee's Greenhouses
55 North St.
Danielson, CT 06239

Lyon, Lyndon
14 Multcher St.
Dolgeville, NY 13329

Merry Gardens
Camden, ME 04843

Oak Hill Gardens
Binnie Road
Dundee, IL 60118

Tinari Greenhouses
2325 Valley Rd.
Huntington Valley, PA
19006

✍ ✍ Botanical Name/Common Name Cross Reference

Botanical Name	Common Name
Acalypha	Chenile plant
Agapanthus	Lily-of-the-Nile
Agave	Century plant
Allium	Flowering onion
Begonia 'Crestabruchii'	Lettuce begonia
Begonia erythrophylla	Beefsteak begonia
Begonia 'Maphil'	Cleopatra begonia
Beloperone guttata	Shrimp plant
Billbergia nutans	Queens tears
Campanula	Bellflower
Capsicum	Pepper plant
Chamaedorea erumpens	Bamboo palm
Daphne odorata	Fragrant Daphne
Echinocactus grusoni	Barrel cactus
Eranthemum nervosum	Blue sage
Eucharis grandiflores	Amazon lily
Eucomis	Pineapple lily
Euphorbia pulcherrima	Poinsettia
Fatshedera lizei	Tree ivy
Fatsia japonica	Japanese fatsia
Guzmania monostachia	Red hot poker plant
Haemanthus	Blood lily
Hippeastrum	Amaryllis
Howea forsteriana	Paradise palm
Hoya carnosa	Wax plant
Ixia	Corn lily
Lycaste aromatica	Cinnamon orchid
Miltonia	Pansy orchid
Neomarica	Apostle plant
Neoregelia spectabilis	Fingernail plant
Nerine	Guernsey lily

Botanical Name	Common Name
Odontoglossum pulchellum	Lily-of-the-Valley orchid
Oncidium ornithorhynchum	Butterfly orchid
Pandanus veitchii	Screw pine
Paphiopedilum callosum	Balinese dancer
Petrea	Queens wreath
Reinwardtia indica	Yellow flax
Rhapis excelsa	Lady palm
Rhipsalis paradoxa	Mistletoe cactus
Rivina humilis	Rouge plant
Sinningia	Gloxinia
Solanum pseudo-capsicum	Jerusalum cherry
Streptocarpus	Cape primrose
Tulbaghia	Society garlic
Vallota	Scarborough lily
Zephyranthes	Rain lily
Zygocactus truncatus	Christmas cactus
Zygocactus truncatus	Easter cactus

♫ ♫ Common Name/Botanical Name Cross Reference

Common Name	Botanical Name
Amaryllis	*Hippeastrum*
Amazon lily	*Eucharis grandiflores*
Apostle plant	*Neomarica*
Balinese dancer	*Paphiopedilum callosum*
Bamboo palm	*Chamaedorea erumpens*
Barrel cactus	*Echinocactus grusoni*
Beefsteak begonia	*Begonia erythrophylla*
Bellflower	Campanula
Blood lily	Haemanthus
Blue sage	Eranthemum nervosum
Butterfly orchid	*Oncidium ornithorhynchum*
Cape primrose	*Streptocarpus*
Century plant	Agave

Common Name	Botanical Name
Chenile plant	Acalypha
Christmas cactus	*Zygocactus truncatus*
Cinnamon orchid	*Lycaste aromatica*
Cleopatra begonia	*Begonia* 'Maphil'
Corn lily	Ixia
Easter cactus	*Zygocactus truncatus*
Fingernail plant	*Neoregelia spectabilis*
Flaming sword	Vreisea splendens
Flowering onion	Allium
Fragrant Daphne	*Daphne odorata*
Gloxinia	Sinningia
Guernsey lily	*Nerine*
Japanese fatsia	*Fatsia japonica*
Jerusalum cherry	*Soldanum pseudo-capsicum*
Lady palm	*Rhapis excelsa*
Lettuce begonia	*Begonia* 'Crestabruchii'
Lily-of-the-Nile	Agapanthus
Lily-of-the-Valley orchid	*Odontoglossum pulchellum*
Mistletoe cactus	*Rhipsalis paradoxa*
Pansy orchid	Miltonia
Paradise palm	*Howea forsteriana*
Pepper plant	*Capsicum*
Pineapple lily	Eucomis
Poinsettia	*Euphorbia pulcherrima*
Queen's tears	*Billbergia nutans*
Queen's wreath	Petrea
Rain lily	*Zephyranthes*
Red hot poker plant	Guzmania monostachia
Rouge plant	*Rivina humilis*
Scarborough lily	Vallota
Screw pine	*Pandanus veitchii*
Shrimp plant	*Beloperone guttata*
Society garlic	*Tulbaghia*

Common Name	Botanical Name
Tree ivy	*Fatshedera lizei*
Wax plant	*Hoya carnosa*
Yellow flax	*Reinwardtia indica*

Index

163